Frontline Woman

D0068215

LaCinda Bloomfield

Copyright © 2019
LaCinda Bloomfield Communications.

Disclaimer

The events and conversations in this book have been set down to the best of the author's ability, although some names and details have been changed to protect the privacy of individuals.

FRONTLINE WOMAN

Table of Contents

TO ALL FRONTLINE WOMEN
who have paved the way for our greatness,
both in heaven and on earth, and to those still yet
to arrive...

May we live our lives as legends.

We don't fear the danger—
WE ARE THE DANGER!

Cover Photo was taken at the temples of Angkor Wat in
Siem Reap, Cambodia. I was honored to join a company of
female Pastors and leaders on a mission of mercy to the
children who are victims of human trafficking.

Introduction

FINDING THE FRONTLINE

"Just send me her number... I need to talk to her now!" She answers my call—with silence... "Sweetheart you don't need to say a thing. Just let me pray for you..."

I begin praying for a precious woman who cannot speak because of profound emotional grief.

This young lady had received the news years ago that the chances of her conceiving a child were highly unlikely... but she loved kids, and she desperately wanted to be a mommy, so after many tears, she began to pray.

Out of her deep sense of loss, she felt that God was directing her to take her love for children and become a Foster-mom for His precious kids who have been removed from their families and placed in the system. They so desperately need love and a stable family home. So this ordinary woman bravely took on the extraordinary challenge of fostering hurting young children.

One of her foster girls who I'll call *Mary* became a "heart-child". Mary and her new mom looked and acted so much alike that you'd swear they were biological mother and daughter, and they accomplished so much together. This bright little girl faced so many issues, but her foster mom believed in her. She took her from a terrible beginning to a stable life of love and the promise of a brilliant future ahead.

Naturally, the mom applied for adoption, and all the pieces fell into place for her temporary care of Mary to turn into a permanent family arrangement. Just as the papers were going through, in the last days of processing, our foster-mama received a call...

Everything came to a screeching halt. Someone had put a stop to the adoption. As unfortunately sometimes happens, in a last-minute decision, her sweet little almost-daughter would be taken from her and given to the child's family member, someone who did not have a good record and was part of the reason she was in the fostering system in the first place.

Talk about utter heartbreak... She couldn't even speak... Just sobs and deep breaths were all I heard as I continued...

Authority and power came all over me. It was not to stop the situation, but it was to strengthen this foster-mama in her higher call to greatness. It was to reassure her of God's ASSIGNMENT to parent His children in DESPERATE need, despite the risk of heartache.

God's higher calling is not for the faint of heart but for those who will stand bravely in the face of injustice, and dare to do something about it—and no matter what, never back down!

I took a deep breath and God's voice FORCEFULLY rang through me...

"You are NOT called to the easy, the comfortable, the simple... You are called HIGHER to a place of TRUST, RESPONSIBILITY, and INFLUENCE. It takes courage, steadfast faith, and a brave heart! Your Father in heaven has called you to the extraordinary, the miraculous, to the no-turning-back life! YOU are a FRONTLINE woman. You know your Master's voice; you know your message, and you know your mission. STAND your ground and don't lose your footing. You are DANGER to injustice! You CAN do this! You CAN walk this out! God is with you ALWAYS."

As I hung up, 'FRONTLINE WOMAN' was born in my heart...

I felt God's voice all over it, and He ministered it to me immediately. I had never heard the term 'FRONTLINE WOMAN' before, but as I said it out loud, I felt the power of God.

I ran for my Bible, and it opened straight up to a scripture God placed in my heart years ago, but I never quite understood. For several years my Bible would crack right open to it. Over and over again, I'd read it, and pray about it, and I'd hold it close to my heart. But this time I GOT IT! It captivated me. It changed me forever....

"Jesus continued according to plan, traveled from town to town, village after village, preaching God's kingdom. The Twelve were with him. There were also some women in their company who had been healed of various evil afflictions and illnesses: Mary, the one called Magdalene, from whom seven

demons had gone out; Joanna, wife of Chuza, Herod's manager; and Susanna—along with many others who used their considerable means to provide for the company."

Luke 8:1-3 (MSG)

As I held God's Word in my hand, I heard Him speaking deeply...

"IT IS TIME FOR A REVOLUTION OF MY WOMEN TO RISE UP and LEAD WITH LOVE ON THE FRONTLINE OF INJUSTICE.

I'm asking you to challenge My women to say YES to their HIGHER calling of TRUST, RESPONSIBILITY, and INFLUENCE I've placed on their life."

FRONTLINE:—THOSE WHO ARE CLOSEST TO THE ENEMY

Now, you need to know, I'm absolutely a total NOBODY. I'm just an ordinary girl like you, who chose to say a passionate YES to my Savior Jesus Christ, despite the many painful disappointments and deep emotional pain I have endured.

It was an easy YES because I fully... Know My Master, know His Message, and I know My Mission.

And He's calling you now. Oh, answer YES to the extraordinary so you can experience something you've never experienced before! Miraculous adventures always happen outside the comfort zone of ordinary... You are NOT ordinary in Christ Jesus — You are MORE THAN A CONQUEROR!

I KNOW you are ASKING, PRAYING, CRAVING TO SERVE HIM MORE... I can sense your YES to a CHANCE like no other, since your first yes to Jesus.

You are accepting the HIGHER call that your Savior has beckoned you to, and there is NOTHING like it. The Revolution within you has begun!

The FRONTLINE embraces those who are strong enough to be closest to the enemy, the woman who has become SO strong, the enemy is no longer intimidating to her. She has her own unique place of FAITH ON THE FRONTLINE!

For those who are already positioned on the FRONTLINE yet discouraged and disheartened because the fight is getting long and hard, just know that this is your time to receive tremendous encouragement, fresh insight, and renewed hope.

You are strategically placed on the FRONTLINE to make an incredible impact for God, and this is no time for giving up now. In fact, it's time to take an even greater stand! TOGETHER, WE ARE UNSTOPPABLE.

Some of us dream of MORE... We want the FRONTLINE life that God calls us to, but how do we take our place? How do we take our dreams, passions, and visions and turn them into an impactful Frontline ministry?

I frequently get asked can a WOMAN lead, pastor, develop, create, and forge ahead in the church, in the environment of denominational thinking, stubborn mindsets, and male-dominated roles?

What DOES the Bible really say about us female leaders? What if I'm just a mom but I feel called? Is being a wife a calling? What if I'm older... like really older and I feel called?

What if I'm young; how long must I wait to serve God? What if I'm a social media influencer?

What if I love business?

What if I served time in prison, sold my flesh, aborted a child, couldn't stay married— again?

Can ANY female step up and be a FRONTLINE Woman for God?

YES. YES. YES!

As you learn your Master's voice, you will discover your message, and ultimately activate your mission; there's absolutely NO LIMIT to what God will do with YOUR UNIQUE, SPECIAL, BEAUTIFUL, GIFTED life.... A life that is thrusting you right on to the FRONTLINE even now.

God has placed this book in your most capable hands, and He's asking you for all your heart. This is your YES MOMENT.

We get what we BELIEVE, not what we want... Believe now with your FULL HEART because HE LOVES YOU AND HAS CHOSEN YOU to receive everything.

Grab a friend or two or more and let's get started on taking up your own special place on the FRONTLINE. We are unstoppable together!

FRONTLINE DISCUSSION

At the end of each chapter, we will close with FRONTLINE DISCUSSION.

This will be a time of reflection and strengthening for all FRONTLINE Women, those new to the line, and for those who have so lovingly committed themselves to it a long time ago. There is something very tender and beautiful about going back to the beginning and reflecting on your first yes to Jesus.

This is a fantastic group study course... Everything on the FRONTLINE is better together, so gather your tribe and get started. You can meet monthly, weekly, or daily. You can go chapter by chapter for 9 weeks, or you can go section by section for 3 weeks, or you can double the chapters for 5 weeks including the last chapter on week 5.

FRONTLINE WOMAN is being used in small venues like dorm rooms, coffeeshops, church rooms, and large church gatherings in auditoriums.

Women's hearts are being ignited to step onto the FRONTLINE without hesitation and embrace the adventure they may only have dreamed about. Many churches have invited me to kick off their group FRONTLINE study, or they have asked me to be the ending guest of their time to celebrate their completion. Either way, I'm happy to be a blessing to you in any way I can.

Start by registering your group today at FRONTLINEWOMANBOOK.COM. You'll be offered more resources and ideas for making your FRONTLINE group an experience to remember.

I recommend that each girl have her own FRONTLINE WOMAN book so she can fully experience the power behind the message and have her own written words following each chapter. However, if someone honestly cannot afford one, then I give full permission to make copies of the FRONTLINE DISCUSSION sections of each chapter. I don't want anyone to miss out.

Let's get started together.

I believe in you,

LaCinda xoxo

Chapter One

MEET YOUR MASTER

"Master, you don't have to go to all this trouble.
I'm not that good of a person, you know.
I'd be embarrassed for you to come to my house,
even embarrassed to come to you in person."

Luke 7:6-8 (MSG)

There is nothing quite like the day you meet your Master, Jesus Christ. He has no hesitation showing up in your life, regardless of who you are, what you've done, or where you've been. I don't (yet) know how He found you, but I want to tell you how He found me.

My parents felt like they needed God in their lives, so they started attending a small Baptist church. The church didn't have a pulpit, so my dad offered to build them one. They were thrilled!

My dad measured the Pastor's height, he chose beautiful wood, and every night after work in the back of our kitchen (because we didn't have a garage) he worked on building the pulpit.

My mom was one special lady. She never complained once that there was a huge wooden block in the kitchen and dust everywhere as my dad sanded away, even letting me do little things to help. It was looking beautiful and almost complete.

One evening there was a knock on our door and three men wearing suits showed up. After talking to my parents, my mom fell back into her chair and started to cry. When they left, I patted my mommy in my 4-year-old way and said, "What's wrong, why you cry'n Mama?" She looked at me and in her sweet dramatic way said, "The church won't take daddy's pulpit because he smoooookes!" I was utterly heartbroken. Even in my young mind, I knew exactly what it all meant. Since my daddy smoked, they refused to have his *unholy* pulpit on their platform. My home was sad and bewildered for weeks. My little family of three was rejected and deeply hurt... We were outcasts.

JESUS WAS REVOLUTIONARY

Jesus was a Rabbi, and Rabbis in His day would go to the fancy synagogues and beautiful temples and preach to the best of the best. The Rabbis were known as Masters because they had mastered the learning of the law. Young well-studied men would pick a Rabbi and follow him hoping he would choose them as one of his team. They would flaunt their impressive spiritual abilities to quote and interpret scripture and prove that they came from affluent families with wealth and position.

Jesus was revolutionary. Instead of impressing people at the temple and looking for the best of the best, Jesus went to the shore of Galilee to preach. Vast crowds of ordinary men, women, and children gathered. Jesus stepped onto a fishing boat so His voice could carry across the water and everyone could hear His teaching.

When He floated back to shore, He turned to the dirty fishermen with smelly scales on their hands and rough sunburnt skin. These fishermen had no fancy tunics, no articulate knowledge of the law, and no refined etiquette, but Jesus went over to them. He went to where they were doing life, and He joined them.

Can you imagine what it must have been like for a Rabbi to walk over to their part of the shore in his white priestly robes and actually talk to them, value them, and then want to take them out to catch fish, A LOT OF FISH... What a moment of never being the same again.

Jesus then, simply asked them, "Will you follow me?"

Can you feel in your heart for a moment what it felt like for sandy-footed men who fished for a living to hear Jesus ask this revolutionary question? "WILL YOU FOLLOW ME?"

"Who us? You mean you would choose us to be your followers? We never dreamed of such a high calling. Our families are not rich, we have nothing to bring you. We wouldn't even be fishermen if we were better schooled in the scriptures and the ways of the temple... Master look at us, you know who we are!" (see Luke 5:1-11)

Yes, Jesus knows exactly who you are. He knows you, and He knows right where you are too.

He knew me.

I was the little girl who was being sexually abused by the older neighbor girl who lived down the street. It was horribly humiliating abuse, and I experienced hideous nightmares and terrible self-hate even at such a young age. I became very fearful, angry, and mean.

During this time, I went to have my tonsils out. As the surgery was underway, something unexplainable happened.

All I know is, I left my body. I drifted up toward the ceiling, and as I looked down at myself, I saw the huge silver light dome over my upper body and three people dressed in dark green rushing around me. I was floating up, high in the air.

All my emotional pain was gone, and I felt SO MUCH LOVE. I was free, with absolutely no fear. I turned to go towards a massive glowing swirl of sparkling light over to the side where the ceiling and wall met when a voice, neither male nor female said, "Go back, Cindy." I answered, "No, I don't want to, I like it up here and I want to stay." Again, the voice sternly said, "Cindy, GO BACK NOW!" Suddenly, an enormous force like an ocean wave swept over me. I remember gasping a deep breath as it pushed me down and that was it, I was under anesthesia again.

My surgery took hours, and my mom said when the doctor finally came out, he was white as a sheet as he sat down with my parents. He was quite upset, and he told my parents he couldn't stop the bleeding, and they almost lost me. They also removed my adenoids, which is what gave him all the trouble. He was deeply concerned and kept me in the hospital for several extra days. My mom says I woke up whispering to her about my experience even though it was painful for me to talk, and to this day it's still a very vivid memory.

A night or so after being home from the hospital, my parents heard me choking in my sleep. Somehow, I had burst the stitches open in my nose, and I was covered in blood. I distinctly remember feeling so weak and cold. I shivered, as my mom bundled me up in a big blanket. She held me as my dad frantically drove back to the hospital in the middle of the night.

This time, I was there for over a week. I cried at night, and the precious nurses would rock me back to sleep. They were dressed in their old-fashioned, well-starched uniforms, immaculate white nylon stockings, and pointed nurses hats.

It was the late 60s and back then great comfort came from singing hymns. They would gently sing songs to me about Jesus as I drifted back to sleep. I'll never forget the love they gave me.

Not too long after I had finally recovered, I was out on my tricycle when a pretty teen girl walked up and handed me a flyer. She kindly told me to take it to my mommy, and she hoped she'd see me at her church next week. My mom looked at it and said, "Cindy, you need to go to this. It's called Vacation Bible School." It sounded good to me, so I got excited.

My Mom drove me to a curb inside the church's parking lot and said, "You see right here where I'm dropping you off? You come right out here to this spot because I don't want to have to go into the church and get you." Understandably at this point, my parents were very hurt and wanted nothing to do with the church for themselves, but they still wanted me to experience God.

I walked in alone; I was scared but deep down inside I was not going to let anything stop me, so I bravely went in.

It was wonderful. The teachers were like the nurses who rocked me back to sleep in the hospital; they were older, kind, and so loving.

The helpers were young and happy. We even sang a song about being happy because Jesus was our friend! It was quite the concept in my young mind that 'Jesus makes you happy.'

At story time we all had to fold our hands and get quiet.

A precious lady stood in front of a big felt board. She lovingly told the salvation story of Jesus, taking characters from her open Bible and carefully placing each one on the board...

She put up a black heart and talked about sin, pain, and hurt, which I knew well. Then she placed a red heart over the black heart and spoke right to us in the present tense, "Jesus knows you are not always good, and bad things happen, but He wants you to know today He loves you just as you are. Jesus knew you needed a Savior, so He chose to die on the cross and shed drops of blood just for you."

Finally, she placed a white heart over the red heart, and then added a big cutout of Jesus on the cross, as she reached up to the top of the board and flipped a black light on, and Jesus glowed with the white heart next to him.

At that moment, it was just me and Jesus. No one else was in the room.

In my little mind of reason, somehow the way the board glowed reminded me of the bright swirling light I had seen during surgery. All my anger melted away, and at almost 5 years old, I began to cry. The teacher said, "You see when Jesus comes into your heart, He washes it white as sparkling snow. If you want to ask Jesus to come into your heart, then come to the front." I *ran.*

They instructed us to kneel, so with my knees to the floor, and my little blonde head bowed down I began to sob... All my broken heart kept saying was, "I LOVE YOU JESUS, I LOVE YOU."

A sweet lady gently helped me up and took me to the Pastor's office off to the side of the large beautiful sanctuary. I was so emotional.

How do you tell an adult, "I'm being abused, my family got kicked out of a church, I think I recently died, I was in the hospital for a loooooong time (to a kid), I'm having terrible nightmares, I'm afraid of everything, and I hate myself?"

Jesus knew. I knew that for sure. He came right down to the sandy shore of my little fearful shattered heart and said, "I'm here... Will you follow Me?"

I repeated a prayer and wholeheartedly said yes to Jesus as this sweet older lady named Hilda wrapped her arms around me and hugged me.

Jesus met my mom that day too. I heard her voice coming down the hallway. Oh no... I was supposed to go to the car....

"What is going on?" She said.

The actual Pastor came out of a side door and introduced himself to my mom. Hilda told her, "Mrs. McCoy, your daughter asked Jesus into her heart today, and she was very serious about it, and you need to know she had a very emotional experience."

Hilda reached out to my mom and invited her to sit down. My mom opened up to her about our church life experience, and Hilda reassured her we were welcome to come to this church.

My mom left that afternoon so happy, feeling excepted with a renewed hope that God's House may just have a place for our family after all.

When you meet Jesus Christ, you are never the same again. Something special happens just between you and Him. All of who you are becomes neutralized by all of who He is. It revolutionizes you and leaves you craving to know Him more.

The next day at VBS there was an AMAZING special guest Ventriloquist, Bob Bradford, and his puppet Jiggers Johnson. They were fantastic, and it mesmerized me!

That Friday night we had to bring our parents to the big closing rally. In fact, whoever brought the most friends that night would actually get to put Jiggers Johnson on their lap for a Polaroid photo (your picture slowly appeared on a thin plastic square right before your eyes, which was as cool as your first iPhone!) I demanded my parents take all my friends and me. I personally got on our home rotary telephone, my mom helped me dial the numbers, and I invited everyone I could think of.

Friday night came and there we were... Me, my parents, and my friends....

"If you brought more than five friends, stand up with your friends so we can count them."

I was overjoyed as I motioned to all my friends to stand up... When they got to me to count my friends they said, "Oh, no little girl... your friends have to be kids!" WHAT?? No one mentioned that part!

I'm an only child, and my "friends" were all my parent's friends—adults!

That took me down to only one kid-friend, and so I lost the chance to have Jiggers sit on my lap.

I sat back and watched as another little boy put Jiggers on his lap, and I was so sad... Well, mad actually! At that moment I decided I needed my own dummy-doll for my own lap to tell people about Jesus too!!

When you meet your Master, you can't wait to find a way to serve Him, and you realize that others need to know Him too. A deep desire flames up inside and you become consumed with what consumes Him... lost, broken, hurting people... Just like you.

Like the Samaritan woman who Jesus found at the well... She could not keep quiet! (*see* Mark4)

My parents purchased the "Bob & Jiggers" record album for me that night, and I played it nonstop! I emulated every detail, voice, and song. Every part that Jiggers had, I wouldn't move my lips, and I developed a cute little puppet voice.

All I could imagine was being on a stage somewhere with my puppet telling others about Jesus just like Bob and Jiggers. I didn't have a puppet, so of course, all my dolls had voices and personalities.

We found a plastic ventriloquist doll at a store called Dooly's in downtown Long Beach. He was $16 bucks which was not cheap at the time, especially for a little kid. I prayed for the money daily. On my 5th birthday, I received all I needed, so we went, and I purchased "Willy Talk" which was printed on his red velvet shirt.

My dad helped me to learn to "throw my voice" which meant learning how to force out my breath which would make my voice louder, so it sounded like the doll was talking. It worked great because you would use your normal voice to speak to the puppet and a forceful voice to answer yourself without moving your lips.

It's a great illusion and not as simple as you might think, especially for such a young little girl.

During this time my parents recommitted their lives to Jesus. They officially joined our new church family, and Hilda became my Sunday School teacher. She loved me; she took me places and invested a lot in me. She greatly changed my life, and when I get to heaven, I can't wait to hug her.

My parents soon became involved in children's ministry and helping with the youth. My dad also served on the usher team, and my mom was busy with all kinds of projects at the church. We were there a lot, and I loved it. We also moved into the first home we ever owned, which took me away from the girl who was hurting me, and the abuse stopped abruptly.

I practiced ventriloquism daily and became really good with Willy Talk. Before long, I was being asked to perform in other churches, schools, Girl and Boy Scouts, hospitals, and so many other places. People got a kick over this little kid and her puppet. GOD WILL USE ANYTHING YOU GIVE HIM TO LOVE HIS PEOPLE!

Doors were continually opening for us. My favorite became going to the "old folks' homes." The older people just loved us, and I loved all of them. They were SO lonely, and it always greatly touched me. I was a missionary in my heart and would tell everyone I could about Jesus, with or without my doll.

THE MASTER WILL SET WRONGS RIGHT

When you become His, you join the company of believers who connect in spreading His Love. Unfortunately, it often gets messed it up with religion, rules, and regulations, but your Master will make it right. We MUST NOT let people's mistakes keep us from joining His company of Frontline believers. If someone has hurt you, and it's caused you to step away from your Master's following, be courageous and STEP BACK IN!

My parents made friends with some sweet Hispanic people in our new church. They were a big family, and THEY LOVED JESUS AND

'SAVING SOULS' as we used to call it back in those days.

One night they were all visiting our home when my dad asked, "What's in that big garage over on the church property?" They went to the Pastor and found out it was a broken-down bus. My dad said, "Well, let's fix it!" It wasn't long before he got it up and running. It was a beautiful bus—but an empty bus.

Our friends said, "No problem, let's fill it. Come on, we'll take you out, door-to-door and invite kids and their families and bring them to church."

So, we went door-to-door on Saturday mornings inviting kids to come to church on the bus, and leading people to Jesus. Before long, neighborhood kids were filling the bus each Sunday. I learned how to really love broken people on that bus. My parents were heroes to so many, they were legends!! Everyone loved Mr. Dave & Mrs. Marilyn McCoy.

As the next Vacation Bible School approached, my mom realized all our bussed kids wouldn't be able to come without the bus. My dad had to work during the day, so she decided she'd get her bus license. She practiced a lot, passed the test, and off we went to get all our kids for Vacation Bible School.

Looking back, HOW BRAVE! HOW COURAGEOUS! That was one BIG bus, but the NEED was great, and a FRONTLINE WOMAN was added to the company that day.

It thrilled our Pastor, and the church was ecstatic! It was amazing how it built so much momentum each day as all the kids from all over our city filed into God's House. There were so many hurting sad and *hungry* kids that my mom made snack bags for them all because so few had eaten breakfast. She even packed a hairbrush and had a bus-helper comb their hair.

When you've met your Master, you become like Him. You realize you are His answer. You are His mind to figure this all out, His eyes to see into the needs, His voice to speak His love, His back to carry the weight, His heart to bring compassion, His hand to extend help, His wallet ready with resources, and His feet to carry it out. (taken from my book, "Discover Your Creative Expression.")

One evening our friends came over to our home, and my parents shared their hurtful story about the pulpit. Our friends asked, "Where's the pulpit now?"

They got SO EXCITED WHEN THEY HEARD MY DAD HAD IT STORED AWAY.

They said... "We are taking both of you and Cindy to Mexico! We have a church there desperately NEEDING A PULPIT and Cindy can bring her puppet." Typing this now brings tears to my eyes! We all had a "glory hallelujah time" in that kitchen on Rose Avenue in Long Beach, California (my childhood home, until I was 13).

I will hold in my heart forever the day when we loaded that big beautiful pulpit into our station wagon and piled clothes, toys, food, and blankets on top. We drove in a big caravan to Mexico!

I joined in the company of women who traveled with Jesus, town after town, village after village, preaching God's kingdom, spreading the Message (Luke 8:1-3).

It is as vivid in my mind as if it happened yesterday when I lifted Willy Talk up and sat him on the edge of the pulpit my dad (and I) had built in that old kitchen of ours.

Now—that pulpit was sitting on the platform of a precious Mexican church. Little Willie Talk said, "Hola, Yo tengo gozo en mi corazón" without moving my lips! (Hello! I've got joy in my heart) The crowd went crazy and got so happy!! I sang them a song I'd learned in Spanish about having Jesus in my heart, and it gives me joy! News spread quickly and I went from church to church for four days. I was in heaven.

I had met my Master, joined His company of followers, and we were off...

I became a FRONTLINE GIRL.

FRONTLINE DISCUSSION

Reframe in your mind when you met your Master from the perspective of "He Chose You!" He walked to the shore of your life and asked, "Will you follow me?"

Write out how it felt from your emotional perspective. Go right back to the season of your salvation and experience it anew. Give it detail, color, and flair. See the full picture in your mind. Cry if you need to, but experience your Master choosing you all over again.

"You didn't choose me, remember; I chose you, and put you in the world to bear fruit, fruit that won't spoil. As fruit bearers, whatever you ask the Father in relation to me, he gives you."

John 15:16 (MSG)

Remember, Jesus chose his team, they did not choose Him. They were not young future Rabbis competing for position, living the dream life of prestige and honor. They were hardworking fisherman, making nets in the hot sun, when Jesus walked right up to them. Don't you ever wonder why some average guys who fished for a living would drop everything for a teacher?

... BECAUSE IT WAS AN HONOR TO BE CHOSEN BY A RABBI—LET ALONE THE MASTER JESUS CHRIST!

WHEN I MET MY MASTER....

If you are in a group, choose someone and share with one another in testimony style your salvation stories. Tell it with feeling and heart. If you are meeting together weekly, consider picking one or two at each gathering to share their season of salvation story.

You can read it or share it from memory but most importantly let it flow from your heart with emotional backing. (Consider a set amount of time for sharing your stories so your meeting does not go too long.)

FRONTLINE PRAYER

"Dear Heavenly Father, thank You for choosing me. You have come to the shores of my life and loved me right where I am. I ask now that You completely cleanse me as we begin a fresh season together. Renew a right, good, strong, spirit within me. I confess anything I have between You and I, that is keeping me from allowing You into every area of my life. I ask that You cleanse my memory of the past and I pray that You give me new thoughts about who I am in You, Christ Jesus....

I love You and thank You for _____ Amen."

FRONTLINE CONFESSION

"I accept the call of my Master Jesus Christ, and I say yes to the FRONTLINE life that He has entrusted me to. I will serve Him with my whole heart and commit my life fully to Him. I let all undeserving thoughts and actions go as I embrace who God has created me to be. I receive all of God's blessing for my life, and I prepare my heart now for what He wants to build in me through this FRONTLINE Book season."

SCRIPTURES TO BUILD YOUR FAITH

John 3:16-21; Romans 10:9-13

Ephesians 2:8-9; Psalm 62:5-8

Jeremiah 17:7-8; Romans 8:38-39

Chapter Two

KNOW YOUR MASTER

Jesus went from the city of Galilee to find his cousin John, the baptizer, at the Jordan river. When Jesus found John, he resisted and said, "Jesus, no! You should baptize me."

Jesus answered, "John, it's proper for you to do this to fulfill the Word." So John consented as baptism was the custom to celebrate a Rabbi's entrance into ministry. Many gathered around to watch this new Rabbi's baptism take place.

John took Jesus into his hands and thrust Him under the water, and as Jesus splashed up, miraculously the skies burst open, and like an actual dove, the Holy Spirit came upon Jesus, as His Father's voice announced, "This is My Beloved Son

Jesus, My Chosen One... Listen to Him!" (Matthew 3:13-17)

God's voice booms from heaven as a stunning white dove drops down and flutters on the shoulders of Jesus, and the crowd that had gathered, witness a profound moment of not just a Rabbi's baptism but THE SON OF GOD'S baptism...

"He is here! The Son of God is here." News spread quickly, and you can paint in your mind the beautiful experience of exactly how your Savior became the MASTER of all... Jesus, your Master, the Son of the living God.

Your Master Jesus Christ chose you... Just as He chose His traveling company, Mary of Magdalene, Joanna, Susanna, and the many others who Jesus valued, each in their own unique ways. Jesus invited them, loved them, healed them, and placed them into His company. He taught them His ways which were so different from the ways of the current culture. He took who they were and who they had become because of Him, and He guided them to the FRONTLINE with Him.

Jesus, your Master, knows the deep secret places within your heart, and He's here right now wanting to reveal more of His heart to yours. Just as He sat with His disciples and the company of women that followed Him and taught them His ways to empower them for the FRONTLINE, He is enabling you now.

He wants you to understand a tender topic that's still evolving... YOU, as a WOMAN IN MINISTRY. Your Master is here to set you free to minister with confidence on the FRONTLINE.

Your Heavenly Father masterfully, with beautiful intention, created you female. His immeasurable value upon you as a WOMAN is limitless. He fashioned you as a "Help-mate" and there is something very precious to Jesus when a woman acknowledges and understands that God has gifted her as *His* helpmate here on earth (Genesis 2:18-25). Helpmate is a term that simply means "bringing completeness" or "fully complementing" the masculine here on earth.

I love the explanations; "An equal and perfect counterpart," and "If one could do it all—why would we need the other?"

We as women bring balance, stability, and wholeness to the men God has gifted us to.

I must say to you with my whole heart, I HONOR MEN. And I'm asking you sincerely to please honor every single man you are graced to serve with too.

This chapter is not telling you that Jesus wants you to rise up over men to do what you are called to do (because anything a man can do, we can do better—NO!) Remember we are bringing balance and completeness to one another, not competing with each other. Let's take some time to understand a few very crucial issues on men AND women in ministry.

You see... I have often received messages and had tearful talks about how the church world rejects, suppresses, and even gets aggressively angry towards women who answer the call to lead in ministry positions. Many non-denominational settings are open to women leading and if you are graced to be in that kind of ministry you are so blessed, however, some of us still have a long way to go in softening hearts towards women leading in many church cultures...

I fully believe a new day is upon God's church as mindsets are changing and the church is advancing. Women are embracing God's call on their life, and men are recognizing how women DO bring balance and stability to their ministries. The result is the church is gaining momentum as God uses everyone in advancing His Kingdom here on earth.

So, I find myself continually helping women of all ages to navigate the mobilization of the female community of Christian leaders willing to say "YES" to their Master. I think God has opened this door to me personally because at an early age He taught me how to gracefully walk the path of being a female leader and then a Pastor. Looking back, I see how God uses everything for each of our ministries on the FRONTLINE.

In my childhood days of the 60s & 70s, a woman could serve in the kid's department, play the piano, and sing in church. She could also be in the office, answering phones, and that was it!

Oh, and as I shared in the last chapter, she could be a bus driver :)) which was revolutionary at that time and was quite the rising up of a woman within our church family.

Once my mom felt God speak to her, she kindly went to our Pastor and asked him what he thought about her getting her bus driver's license and picking up kids for VBS. He told her he had to think it over and then a short time later he got back to her with a thumbs up. Everyone was so excited when we pulled up with a full bus packed with kids for VBS to learn about Jesus.

I fully remember looking up at mom as I climbed the big steps into the massive church bus. It was really something looking up at her sitting in the high driver's seat with the huge steering wheel in front of her. I thought how odd it looked to see her in that position.

She had such a BIG personality, and her happiness FILLED that big ol' bus. It shifted something in me, and I honestly think it embedded the belief that nothing is too hard to do for God— not just as a woman but as a follower of Jesus Christ. I think I told every child three times, "That's MY mom!" as the kids answered me, "We know who Ms. Marilyn is!"

They wanted to feel they had a part of her life too... She knew EVERY ONE of their names and they knew she loved them as well... AND BELIEVE ME, SHE DID.

LOVE FOR LEADING

Both of my parents had fully dedicated their lives to Jesus and become very involved in the church, and then, I seem to remember the leadership changing.

One Sunday my dad came into my Sunday School class and abruptly pulled me out. He was very upset. He had been helping with seating people for Sunday morning services when a man said, "We all need to talk." So, they got together, and the man said, "You see that girl over there, look at her in her short skirt!" (Well, it was the late 60s, and modern fashion was the short 'Go-Go' mini skirt. However, IF you knew better, you sure wouldn't wear one to church.)

The 'holy' men decided to go pull her from the back row and make her leave because *she should have known better than to show up looking like that to church.* My father became irate and begged them to leave her alone.

We as a family had been going door-to-door consistently each Saturday, and we experienced the 'real world' in our community as we knocked on doors and saw what was behind them. It was dark and sad, and many were desperate to know Jesus. 'When you go fishing, you let Jesus clean the fish.'

However, these were VERY different times. My dad said, "I want nothing to do with this." He immediately went to find my mom, grabbed me, and put us in the car, and THAT WAS IT! We were once in the 'Go-Go' girl's place of being kicked out of God's house, and we were not going to have any part of it—so we were out!

My mom heard about a 'wild' on-fire church close to our home. We lived in Long Beach, a suburb of Los Angeles, and in those days you were either a *Go-Go* girl with knee-high boots, high ratted hair with a flip, frosted pink lipstick and thick fashion lashes, or you were a *Hippy-Girl* with no makeup, stringy hair, long maxi-dresses and if you were really cool, you drove a beetle bug with a big yellow daisy flower on the back windshield that had a peace sign in the middle. In Los Angeles whatever you did, you did it ALL the way!

Well, this local church was FULL of Hippies and Go-Go Girls who had found Jesus and were radically on fire with the UNCONDITIONAL LOVE of God.

There was one BIG challenge... The Pastor was not what you'd think.... The Pastor was a WOMAN... A female Pastor, and every Pastor from almost everywhere HATED HER.

Her name was Esther Mallet, and she became my Beloved Pastor. She was a FRONTLINE WOMAN in every way! She gifted me with a LOVE FOR LEADING.

I wish you could have known this pioneer. She LOVED absolutely EVERYBODY. The bikers, the drug addicts, the prostitutes, the go-go girls, the hippies, the gang members, the surfers and the little families like mine. Doctors, community leaders, and many highly successful people attended the church too, and Pastor Mallet LOVED US ALL.

I got to experience an AMAZING Jesus movement with my very own life.

Reverend Mallet was older, her smile was broad, she was plump and full of God's generosity... Ughhhh, I'm crying as I write about her. I guess I see, looking back, how utterly much she affected my life.

Pastor Mallet was beautifully immaculate, with a perfectly coiffed dark hairdo, and very loving eyes that melted your heart. She led people to Jesus every single day!

One time I was walking into a church picnic, and I saw Pastor Mallet leaning her short body through the window, way into what we would have called a 'low-rider car', and it was decked out all the way. I ran over to where she was and walked by slowly to get a glimpse of what she was doing. She had her arms outstretched across two gang members, with a hand on each of their chests.

These guys looked scary, with tattoos, black hair nets, and smoke was coming out of the windows. I stood back just behind the men who were there to keep watch over her. I could see the guys in the car and hear them repeating the 'sinners' prayer (as we called it back then). Next thing I knew, she had them lifting their hands, with palms up, and praying in the Spirit. They both had a full Jesus experience with cigarettes lit, big dice hanging from the rear-view mirror and low tires (which gave her the ability to lean way in!)

No one scared Pastor Mallet. No one intimidated her. No one could stop her from loving the lost, and believe me, many tried, and the church just grew all the more.

Pastor Mallet was despised because she was a WOMAN in leadership. Both men and women attacked her relentlessly, but her results were undeniable. The power of God in the church was vibrant and the vision of my own young life to do ministry as a female grew tremendously.

I would play church by preaching outside on a large wooden power line spool my dad brought home from work. I regularly pretended to lead a choir with a thin white conductor's stick, that I had begged to get for my birthday because I wanted to be just like her daughter, Pastor Kay, and direct the choir one day. I held funerals for the pets that died in the neighborhood, and I had a wedding when my doggy was expecting puppies.

As far as I was concerned, I was gonna be a missionary and a Pastor when I grew up.

I attended the school that the church had started and as I grew into a teenager, my best friend and I decided to be a bit crazy. We went to the local store and stole two beers, brought them back to the school and drank them in the church bathroom. I hated the taste, so I poured mine down the toilet, but I acted silly anyway.

Of course, we had to brag about our daring adventure, while we acted drunk, only to end up in Pastor Mallet's office!

This was totally heartbreaking to me... I was scared out of my wits... How could I do this to my Jesus and my beloved Pastor Mallet? She trusted me on her platform and loved when I performed with my ventriloquism doll (by this time I had a large professional dummy-doll named Tecla that I had purchased from Disneyland. She was beautiful, and Pastor Mallet just loved her and used my gift often).

Pastor Mallet had shown me nothing but love and had especially been there for me when my baby sister died during birth. She put on a fur hat over her messy hair (that I had never seen a mess) and showed up, and held my family's hands through the whole devastating ordeal, and now here I sat as one BIG disappointment to her.

Oh... I wish you could have experienced the grace she gave me as I sat in a heap of tears in her immaculate mint green office with plush red carpet (that always smelled absolutely beautiful).

"Cindy, this just isn't you. What happened to make you step out of your calling and do this?" I could only cry and shake my head. I didn't even try to explain myself.

Then she called my mom in. My mom, who had been the church bus driver, was now the Sunday School Superintendent (leader over all the kid's ministries). The instant I saw the tears falling down her cheeks, I realized my actions had hurt who she was in ministry too, and it crushed me even more.

Pastor Mallet settled her right down immediately and talked to her about how precious I was and how God would really use me one day, and that He had great things ahead for my life in ministry. I actually thought, "WHAT? Is she really talking about me?" Pastor Mallet's grace MELTED any desire in me to do anything like that ever again. That's what the grace of God does. It melts the very desire it covers.

I had consequences, but they meant nothing compared to what I allowed God to do within me.

Because of how she believed in me, it deeply solidified my calling to lead in God's House even more. It was not all that long later, and I was leading my first Sunday School class of first-grade girls, and I loved it.

Time went on, and I attended another church-school in 11th Grade. During Bible class, a male teacher started talking terribly about women in ministry in front of the entire high school class. I could NOT help myself, so I raised my hand and kindly said, "I know a really amazing woman Pastor and..." He abruptly interrupted me with intense anger in his voice, "Yeah, I know her too, she's a BLANK- BLANK (I refuse to print it!) and I heard her husband just died of cancer, and I'd die too if I were married to her."

We had quite a heated exchange. His hatred became so forceful that I ran right out. I fled in hot angry tears to the office and called my mom and told her I'd NEVER return to his class, not ever.

Deep in my heart, I decided to never debate with him or anyone ever again. The crazy thing is that teacher died of stomach cancer a short time later. I could not believe it, but within about a year he was gone.

I really wanted to speak at Pastor Mallet's funeral, just for a moment, but I was from the old days, and there were so many who wanted to share their recent memories and give Pastor Mallet honor, that I decided to remain silent.

If I could have spoken, I would have said something like, "What an honor to stand here today as a woman Pastor. I'm forever grateful for the example both Pastor Mallet and her daughter Pastor Kay, showed me in my life as they pioneered the way for me to have it so much easier to be a woman in ministry than they ever had it. They never wavered in their calling, and their courage has carried me almost daily."

Out of everything Pastor Mallet put into me, I have to thank her the most for her passionate love for Jesus and her unconditional love for everyone. She so gracefully taught me never to let anyone's opinion of what God called me to, stop me from serving Him with my whole heart.

Please let Pastor Mallet and Pastor Kay's example as women ministers, when being a woman in ministry took tremendous courage and tenacity, inspire you to serve God fully, regardless of your gender, race, social status or background.

Another INCREDIBLE woman in ministry during my teen life was Judy McKern who was my Youth Pastor. She and her husband Cliff moved from Pastor Mallet's church and planted a church in Texas. Pastors Cliff and Judy took wild heat because she was called a Pastor. Judy had a radio show, and she was viciously harassed, all because she was a FRONTLINE WOMAN. Judy never wavered and with amazing confidence doused her detractors with love.

She strengthened me and impassioned me to serve Jesus as a teen regardless of what anyone thought, and yet all these women had one thing in common; they ALL had fierce honor for men...

It had NOTHING to do with position and everything to do with SERVICE and LOVE for God, for His people and for His House.

On August 24th, 1985 I married an amazing man, Stephen John Bloomfield whose father, Brother Bloomfield (as he is so affectionately called) is a legendary evangelist, and he also had a church in Canada where we started our married life out.

The day came when my husband became the lead Pastor, and that instantly made me a Pastor's wife at 22 years old. From day one my husband said, "You are my Co-Pastor. You've been doing this since a child, and you must step up and lead with me." I honored him and said I'd do anything he needed.

When I said, "Yes" to be his Co-Pastor I did not do anything I wasn't already doing but once I had the title, the attacks began. I have to say the Canadians, in general, were far more accepting of the idea of a female in a ministry position than the Americans seemed to be at the time. However, we received many hateful letters (before social media), and a few other mean-spirited situations happened. Since moving back into the states, it has gotten pretty rough at times, and very heated attacks have occurred.

Early in these days of Pastoring, I was invited to go to a Daisy Washburn Osborn Women's Conference in Oklahoma.

Both she and her AMAZING daughter, LaDonna were integral during the conference, teaching and emulating confidence to me as a woman in ministry. Daisy and her incredible husband, T.L., were pioneers who raised up Pastors and their wives throughout Africa (these were the days when the only travel to Africa was on a ship). T.L. and Daisy learned several of the native languages and taught male Pastors the value of their wives to their ministries. The incredible things these Pastor-couples started to do were revolutionary.

This conference wowed me and exposed me to a massive world of female leaders, and it placed new confidence within me. I was SO encouraged, but I NEVER would want you to hear how people talked about them.

"They are WOMEN! They are _____ _____" I just can't even repeat what was said, seriously! It devastated me... ALL BECAUSE THEY WERE WOMEN.

Somehow, these legends stayed utterly lovely, showing me who was truly right. To this day Reverend LaDonna is a FRONTLINE woman to reckon with!

I must pause here and point out how COURAGEOUS the men are in our world, who like Jesus, value us, give us honor, and encourage us to serve our Master Jesus Christ wholeheartedly.

I thank God for them all the time as I see SO many incredible men who love, promote, encourage, entrust, and even push us women to the FRONTLINE.

However, sadly I've seen the ugly side of all of this too. I've had attacks verbally by men and women; in person, live during my morning radio show, from pulpits, online, in meetings, and blah, blah, blah!   The crazy thing is, I've never even sought to be in a top leadership position, or seen myself as anything other than a girl who fell deeply in love with Jesus. All I wanted to do as a kid was travel around sharing His love with my puppets, and my life in ministry just evolved from there.

Stephen and I chose a long time ago, never to respond to people's attacks, ever, period.

I highly encourage you to do the same... NO DEBATING or DEFENDING. Let God do it. You keep loving, leading, and serving, and trust God to be your defender... You stay close to Jesus, precious ministry girl. He'll see you through.

LEADING TOGETHER

Your Master came to set the oppression of women—right.

He was revolutionary, a renegade and a disrupter of ALL the gender nonsense! Jesus valued women, and it was rare, rebellious, and entirely out of line with current culture. The longest recorded conversation Jesus had with someone in the Bible was with a woman (John 4 — The Samaritan woman at the well).

Today, Jesus would reach out to every precious hand marked 'Me Too' and softly wipe it clean, remove the pain and set each of us free from all the injustice because that's who He is and what He does.

All this freedom in Jesus and His calling in our lives does NOT mean we as women should be pushy, bossy, or rude—GET OUT OF MY WAY women—I HAVE SEEN THIS, WAY TOO MANY TIMES! We were created to be complementary to the men we are honored to lead and serve with.

Oh, please know you'll get SO much more out of leading and serving when you do it with graceful confidence, honor, and respect to the men (and women) who surround your life.

In my book, "Let's Get A Ring On It", I write about how God created us male and female, the same but different... VERY DIFFERENT!

I'm talking about the science behind God's creation of two chemicals—Testosterone and Estrogen, that cause us to be VERY different from one another and yet VERY complimentary to each other. Leading is not about titles, roles or position. It's about calling, gifts, and abilities to lead, and a willingness to love and serve; both male and female together.

It's interesting that the Bible mentions women right alongside men all throughout the Old Testament.

Everyone from Miriam being part of freeing her people from Egypt with her brother Moses, to Deborah the prophetess and judge, full of God's wisdom, who was integral in winning a massive battle alongside the army leader Barak.

From Sarah, the wife of Abraham to Solomon's mother Bathsheba, who despite a very hurtful beginning, was promoted to Queen and became part of the genealogy of Jesus. There are many accounts that Solomon bowed to his mother Bathsheba in court and gave her a seat to rule next to him. Many believe she wrote Proverbs 31 to her son instructing him in choosing his wife.

There is Jehosheba who saved her baby nephew from a vile massacre that wiped out every family member. She saved the bloodline of Israel by strategically grabbing one little boy, Jehoash and barely escaped death. There were Ruth and Boaz, and Queen Esther who saved her people along with her cousin Mordecai. This is just a FEW of the amazing women who served alongside men in the Old Testament.

According to Historians, there was a certain level of respect for women in Old Testament times. (I'm not suggesting for a moment that there was NOT oppression towards women during these times, as there is no comparison to how we live today in Christian based western cultures.)

Biblical scholars point to the significant decline of how women were treated when Jesus arrives in history, compared to Old Testament times.

The New Testament reflects this sharp regression in the value and respect of women in any capacity. According to reputable scholars, it was brought on by the many eastern cultures that established rigid religious rules and regulations, resulting in terrible oppression against women.

So much so that there are detailed accounts that women rarely left their homes without entirely covering themselves and having to be accompanied by a male at all times. Women were possessions, most daughters were sold to the highest dowry and wives could be disregarded at any time.

A woman's 'word' was useless unless a man could verify her entire story. Children were no different, and the reports are astonishing of what someone could do at will to a child.

The Bible does tell us that many people loved their daughters, like the Centurion who came to Jesus to heal his little girl. However, there was a spirit in the land to oppress everyone with nonstop rules, regulations, and interpretations of the law in any way that suited each culture's dominance. God had had enough of all the nonsense. He loved the world so much that the craziness had to stop.

He sent His son Jesus to the world, not to condemn us but to save us, and deliver us from injustice and oppression into FREEDOM.

JESUS ENTERS OUR OPPRESSIVE, BROKEN, HURTING WORLD

Every chance your Master Jesus had, He VALUED women. The only account of Jesus sounding brash to a woman was in Mark 7:24-29. Jesus is resting with his disciples when a Greek woman searches Him out for help, to heal her daughter.

Jesus seemed indifferent to her, but in studying this, He was not disregarding or speaking unlovingly to her. Jesus knew just how to talk to her in terms she would understand within her culture. He valued her and tenderly tells her she has great faith and sends her home to her healed daughter. Over and over the Word of God paints the most beautiful stories for us of His Son Jesus, setting women free.

Recently, right in the middle of my FRONTLINE revelation, I heard the amazing Hillsong Pastor Donna Crouch speaking, and she said, "I must ask, where are all the women who are called to lead? Where are the women stepping up and really doing some incredible things for God? I know there is a few but there should be more, way more."

Pastor Bobbie Houston (who is a LEGENDARY female leader) was hosting Color Women's Conference 2017 when this theme rang loudly... "Where are the women?" God wants to find us, His daughters, in the field ministering for Him. My heart was beating SO fast as once again, I had great confirmation this book must get into your beautiful hands as soon as my fingers could type it out.

I pray you are challenged to know your Master, to know His Heart for you, and how He is entrusting you to RISE UP, to be the FRONTLINE WOMAN you are gifted to be! Don't say, "But I'm a woman..." ever!

You are called to lead... LEAD WITH LOVE, STRENGTH, and DIGNITY! Remember, we are not here to debate anyone, as this gets us nowhere.

It does not matter if you are called to lead kids, Youth, Young adults, Missions, Administration, as a Pastor or whatever capacity you are called to.

ON THE FRONTLINE WE DO NOT PUSH OUR WAY IN

When Esther was chosen Queen and needed to lead her people to freedom, she didn't abruptly or forcefully go to her King with a complaint and panicking fear. She pulled away to pray and fast and get a plan. She SERVED her King with loving care and make him a magnificent feast. Her heart to serve awakened his heart to grant her whatever she wanted... even up to half of his kingdom. Let's learn from Esther and do all we can to keep our heart pure and free from resentment.

You are not here to battle but to SERVE on the FRONTLINE with your whole heart and see the Salvation of your God.

"My dear, dear friends! I love you so much. I do want the very best for you. You make me feel such joy, fill me with

such pride. Don't waver. Stay on track, steady in God. I urge Euodia and Syntyche to iron out their differences and make up. God doesn't want his children holding grudges.

And, oh, yes, Syzygus, since you're right there to help them work things out, do your best with them. These women worked for the Message hand in hand with Clement and me, and with the other veterans—worked as hard as any of us. Remember, their names are also in the Book of Life.

Celebrate God all day, every day. I mean, revel in him! Make it as clear as you can to all you meet that you're on their side, working with them and not against them. Help them see that the Master is about to arrive. He could show up any minute!"

Philippians 4:1-5 (MSG)

FRONTLINE DISCUSSION

Have you been criticized for being a woman in ministry? If so, what happened?

How would you encourage a female leader who was struggling with criticism?

What men can you list who honor your gift and calling?

How can you thank them for their support?

How can you honor them for being revolutionary in their respect for you as a FRONTLINE WOMAN?

Talk it over with a friend and recognize what a blessing it is when we get to serve together in an environment of honor.

IF THERE IS A STRUGGLE WITH THE MEN IN YOUR WORLD

This is a very tender situation and above all, guard your heart against offense. Think of ways you can show them honor for when they DO give you space to lead. Slowly add more to what you do, respectfully. I have women teach their team to thank the male leaders each time it's appropriate, for seeing the importance and value of women's ministry, and other female-led events. This will help to soften their religiously rigid hearts and allow God to speak to them, but when there is a struggle, they get their walls up, and there is no reasoning with a hard heart.

"For we are not fighting against people made of flesh and blood, but against persons without bodies—the evil rulers of the unseen world, those mighty satanic beings and great evil princes of darkness who rule this world; and against huge numbers of wicked spirits in the spirit world."

Ephesians 6:12 (TLB) ((YIKES!! But oh, so true!!))

I fully believe God makes room for your gifts, talents, and abilities. If you are not succeeding, check your approach and adjust your attitude.

Make a plan of action— PRAYER!

I have seen prayer and fasting soften the hardest of hearts.

FRONTLINE PRAYER

"Dear Father in heaven, You created me in my mother's womb with a purpose wrapped within my DNA. I thank You for that purpose, and I fully accept it. I ask that You help me not to let people's opinions of me hinder what You have called me to on the FRONTLINE. Guide me to respect and honor the men You have placed in my life. I am Your helpmate here on earth, and I ask You to bless my husband (or future husband) and my role of honoring him. Help me to have a heart to serve everyone as You make a way for your promotion upon my life. I love You, and I serve You with my WHOLE heart.   In Jesus name, amen."

FRONTLINE CONFESSION

"I take my place on the FRONTLINE for my Master Jesus Christ. I always honor men as my calling is about what needs to be accomplished and not about gender. My motivation is always my heavenly Father's heart and what He needs from me. I never argue about my calling but rather serve more, love more, and give more, as my actions will always reveal more than words."

SCRIPTURE TO BUILD YOUR FAITH

Genesis 2:18-25; Ruth 3:3-11, Romans 16:1-2; Galatians 3:28, Esther 7:1-10; Proverbs 4:23

If you are struggling, email me. I'd love to HELP you navigate through your leadership circumstances.

I believe in you FRONTLINE WOMAN!

Chapter Three

SERVE YOUR MASTER

*He (Jesus) continued according to plan, traveling from town
to town, village after village, preaching God's Kingdom,
spreading the message. The disciples were with him,
including some women who had been healed of various evil
afflictions and illnesses. Mary the one called Magdalene,
from whom seven demons had gone out, Joanna, wife of
Chuza, Herod's manager, and Susanna,
along with many others who used their
considerable means to provide for the company.*

Luke 8:1-3 (MSG)

Look within your heart and imagine the
marvelous sight of the caravan traveling with the
Master. These were difficult traveling times as the

dust swirled, the sun blazed, hot wind chafed their skin, sharp rocks bruised their feet, but these women STEPPED UP regardless of any pushback.

Nothing stopped them as they walked or even rode a mule in long dresses, head coverings, sandals, chapped lips, sunburned cheeks, squinted eyes, and avoiding the desert creepy-crawlers! I don't care how wealthy you were back then, traveling was noted as a tough adventure, but the love in their hearts for their Master gave them endurance, spurred on their creativity, and left them as legends on the pages of God's Word.

You, my beautiful FRONTLINE WOMAN, are part of the grand caravan still today! You are called, town-to-town, village to village, person to person, nation-to-nation, this very day.

YES!!!! IT IS TOUGH WORK

Whoever thinks about the tough work in the beginning? Not me! I just fell in love with my Master and jumped in with both feet... But as we both know the journey is hard, only to arrive and face injustice. But we stand in our moment, and we declare our dedicated YES to the call to rise up and stand up to the pain of the world that Jesus needs us to heal.

Like our Foster Mom in the beginning, who heartbreakingly had to bid farewell to the dream of her forever daughter...

I gave it a while, and it hit me to call her.

"Hello warrior girl, how's it going, being off the battlefield for a while? Yeah, I know, but it's time to dust it off. You've had time to cry it out and mourn the loss, Sweetheart. Pastor Mama is here to remind you that you have other little one's hearts waiting, praying, needing you."

"This call upon your life is a TOUGH one, with no guarantees, but you ARE strong enough. You are entrusted to serve your Master and serve Him you will. We are not giving up! We are NOT quitting! We pick up the Word of God and we will FRONTLINE this together. You have the FULL armor of God, now let's put it on and get on with it."

She said, "I can't believe you called as today marks exactly one month since my girl left!"

"Well, that's just how your Savior works, isn't it?! You are a FRONTLINE WOMAN, so let's get going!"

"We are not among those who shrink back and are lost, but among those who have faith and so are saved."

Hebrews 10:39 (NRSV)

In the company who traveled with Jesus, many women had been healed of various evil afflictions. Mary Magdalene was one, from whom Jesus cast out seven demons. No doubt, Mary had had some very hurtful times to get through before she could serve her Master. Once she met him, she knew she was called to MORE! A higher place of service and purpose! She did not let her past hold her back; neither will you.

I've been through MANY hellish seasons in my life! I flunked, not one grade in school, but two, both second & third. It was devastating, humiliating and ridiculous.

My only sibling died during labor, and we had to bury my baby sister, Deborah Elizabeth, causing me to feel all the lonelier.

I had my heart shattered into a million pieces as I stood with my wedding dress, flowers, cake and a ring tucked under my pillow only to have him show up, break up, drive off, and NEVER see or talk to him again, not to mention being stuck with all the bills.

I've had to fight for my life and endure unbelievable physical pain, I've come to the end of myself many, many times BUT...

LET ME TELL YOU...

The sicker you've been, the more desperate you were, the harder it was, the deeper the depression you felt, the many tears you cried, the helplessness you fought, the utter hopelessness you endured IS THE MORE YOU HAVE TO SERVE YOUR MASTER WITH.

Through all that pain, you became somebody! You grew up. It was the making of you; it was the becoming of the woman you were created to be! Applied pressure refines your usefulness and makes you extraordinarily valuable to the purposes of God.

Can't you just feel yourself rising up even now to SERVE YOUR MASTER JESUS CHRIST?!

Nothing can or will stop you!!! No fear, no discouragement, displacement, rejection, sickness, or misunderstanding can STOP what God will and IS doing in your life today... RIGHT NOW!

Don't you see that the VERY ministry you are called to is often the place you struggle in the MOST!? The biggest attacks are directed right at your FRONTLINE life. The hardest spot is your happiest place when you win. The puddle of tears makes the greatest splash when the weeping is done. The biggest rejection is God's beautiful protection. The steeper the climb, the stronger and more agile you become. You know He's taking out all the junk and purifying something only YOU CAN DO, STRENGTHENING what only you can bring...

It was horrifying as Jochebed heard the terrifying screams of her people as she saw every little Israelite baby boy being slaughtered. She hid her big pregnant belly and prayed to God for deliverance. She gives birth to a son and decides NOT to give in. She makes a basket and pushes baby Moses down the Nile as his older sister Miriam waits for him to float in front of the princess. He's rescued by the Princess and Miriam says, "I know a Hebrew woman who could nurse him for you."

Jochebed's faith not only spares her boy, but she nurses him too! If you are called to stand on the FRONTLINE FOR CHILDREN — STAND and FIGHT for them! BE COURAGEOUS! They NEED you so desperately. God needs you! Never stop! Be it kid's ministry, fostering, adopting, crises centers, overseeing babies in foreign countries, stand and wage war for the love of a child! God will continuously give you plans for rescue, comfort, and deliverance.

It was terrifying for Jael, when Sisera, the commander of the Canaanite army, who had cruelly oppressed her and her people with his nine hundred iron chariots for twenty years, shows right up at her tent home. She invites him in and gives him warm milk and tells him to lay and rest. As he sleeps, she takes her tent peg in one hand and a hammer in the other and drives it through his temple. Deborah, the prophetess, wrote,

"Most blessed of all women is Jael, wife of Heber the Kenite, most blessed of homemaking women."

Judges 5:27 (MSG)

If you're called on the FRONTLINE as a HOMEMAKER, stand and FIGHT FOR YOUR HOME! Be Brave to LEAD your family with strength.

YOU are called to raise your children—not social media, not television, not a neighbor, not their school—YOU are called to RAISE THEM! Never belittle your call to home!

Be the wife you know you've got inside of you! Be the mom God has gifted you to be! You are not just a homemaker; you are on the FRONTLINE serving your Master in your HOME. As for you and your house—You will ALL serve your Master Jesus Christ.

It must have been petrifying for Queen Esther not only to say, "If I die then I die," but to actually know she could very well be strung up, hung and tortured in a horrid way, along with all of God's people. The custom of hanging in those days was barbaric, and she knew what she faced. She needed a strategy, so she FASTED and PRAYED to her God, along with her maids and all who surrounded her. God gave her a brilliant idea, and it worked.

Her people were freed in an AMAZING deliverance out of the hand of the enemy! If you are called to FREE people from the clutches of the enemy; abuse, addiction, poverty, oppression, persecution, homelessness, prostitution, or human trafficking, you need a strategy, a plan of action! Fast and pray, then take your place of deliverance on the FRONTLINE and serve your Master, and free His people! Break the chains right off injustice—You are a FRONTLINE WOMAN.

Without Rahab's unwavering courage to hide the spies, Joshua would not have been able to take down the walls of Jericho as he did. Biblical History records that Rehab was one of the most beautiful women who ever lived. Her beauty was part of her influence. Beauty always is. I can imagine the guards searching for the men she was hiding, becoming intoxicated by her beauty, causing them to believe her when she told them that the spies had left. She knew the effect she had on men. Maybe she found herself in a harlot lifestyle because her virtue was stolen from her?

One thing is for sure, she was one wise woman. She had already heard about the spy's powerful Almighty God and she wanted to believe in Him and have Him spare her entire family's lives. She devised a plan by creating a long red scarlet rope to let the spies down from her window in the dark of night.

Because of her bravery, she and her family were spared. Her beauty and courage also captivated Joshua, who he fell in love with her and married her. Her heroic act is mentioned throughout the Bible, both old and new testament.

She even made it into Jesus's ancestry—WOW!

If you are created beautiful and feminine, use it as an influence for your Master! I regret my many years of hiding behind my beauty when it was one of my most powerful gifts. If you are a beauty-girl, use it. Blog it. Post it. Don't be shy—use it with dignity and purity to bless and inspire the world.

Don't let anyone tell you, you are too cute, too sweet, or all fluff. No... Listen to me, BEAUTY IS POWERFUL! IT HELPED CAVE AND CRUSH THE WALLS OF JERICHO, and it can do the same today! STUNNING GIRLS are needed on the FRONTLINE! Take your place with great courage, serve and shine your lovely beauty for your Master!

Tabitha, a female disciple (whose home was most likely a church) lay dead... Her still body being gently washed and wrapped by her dear friends, and the widows and the poor whom she loved and helped so much. They were crying and deeply mourning her loss.

She was so loved that when some of the disciples heard Peter was close by they ran to get him. Immediately when Peter heard it was Tabitha, he agreed to come at once.

When he arrived, the those who were gathered showed Peter the clothing she had made them with her own hands. He immediately put everyone out and knelt and prayed.

Peter stood and spoke to her mature lifeless body with a commanding voice, "Tabitha, GET UP!" She immediately came to life, and he helped her rise to her feet. Everyone was shocked and overjoyed, and the news spread wildly, causing MANY to turn their hearts to Jesus! Oh, to love so great that your precious life is given back to you.

FRONTLINE WOMEN are AGELESS women who know how to truly love EVERYONE—the widow, the elderly, the poor. Titus tells us mature women are to teach the younger women how to love their husbands and children, how to be virtuous and pure, and how to keep a good house.

You may even know how to bake, sew and knit. PLEASE never think you are too old or obsolete to be used by the Master. Don't assume your day is done! Don't believe what you do is old-fashioned, outdated or not useful.

WE NEED YOUR life experience, baked goods, knitted blankets, sewn quilts and all things homemade! You are SO valuable and So NEEDED.

You are our MATURE FRONTLINE WOMAN, full of wisdom, gifts, and deep LOVE, so please don't hold back from the current generation.

Lydia of Thyatira was a VERY wealthy woman who sold and produced textiles in the color purple. No other part of the world produced such a vibrant stunning deep color, and it was sought after and shipped everywhere. Scholars say Lydia must have had a vibrant personality to pull off such noted business-savvy back in her day.

She discovered the love of Jesus and realized how tired she was of just living for herself. As she came to believe in Jesus with her whole heart, she lived an even bigger, fuller, and more purposeful life.

Its noted Lydia was the first European convert to Christ, and she used her money to spread the gospel far and wide. She must have felt such exhilaration, and yet maybe a little apprehensive, when she first grasped the concept that HER WEALTH COULD BE USED FOR HER MASTER.

She had a gift to make money, and her ability was not just for her and her family but also for a much bigger cause—The cause of Jesus Christ. She hosted the disciples for long periods of time, taking care of their every need and provided whatever it took to spread the gospel. Her rising up as a Christian was the spark that ignited Christianity in her region of the world, and she had the resources to fund its spreading across the earth.

Business-women are FRONTLINE WOMEN.

Without resources how can the work of ministry be accomplished? How can the gospel reach the ends of the earth? How can Missionaries be sent out? Water-wells get built? Pastors preaching far and wide? Hungry children getting fed? Human trafficking eradicated? Churches flourishing? Missions fully accomplished?

Why is it so often that the business-woman feels second best to God's call? We may think a platform is only in an auditorium but your platform, boss-lady is business, and your FRONTLINE is creating resources. CREATE ON! You know you're living for far more than just more stuff—YOU ARE A FRONTLINE BUSINESS GIRL for your Master and His Mission for your life.

It was daunting as sweet, innocent, untouched Mary heard the Angel speak to her.

She was just a teen girl living her life in very tough times. The Romans had taken over her part of the world and were mean, ruthless, and oppressive. Her people kept waiting for the Messiah to show up as scripture had promised to set them free from their despair. Of course, for Mary, scripture was only what she'd been told by the men in her family because as a female she would not have been allowed to study the scripture for herself or go into the temple where it was taught... But God CHOSE her, a young teen girl (it's estimated she was around fourteen years old).

> *"God placed His Son inside of her womb... and she gladly accepted regardless of her tremendous fear, 'I'm bursting with God-news; I'm dancing the song of my Savior God. God took one good look at me, and look what happened—I'm the most fortunate woman on earth!"*

> *Luke 1:46-55 (MSG)*

Mary accepted that she had something powerful inside her that God was birthing into the world. She bravely took on the challenge even though she might very well be killed for it when the man she was engaged to found out. But Mary boldly birthed the Savior in a stable.

She pushed forth and out the promise came—Jesus... One day, He'd grow to bind up the broken-hearted and set the captives free FOREVER.

FRONTLINE WOMEN are YOUNG GIRLS, TEENS, and YOUNG ADULTS who know God has placed something within them for NOW—Not later, but NOW! She rises up to say yes to the simple, the new, the early stages of the conception of the dream that's within her. She keeps busy serving her Master as He develops and matures her.

I was ministering on the church platform at six years old... I walked out onto a stage, and my puppet sang for Jesus. God developed me from there. Never hold your child back.

Never hold your message back because you are young! Write your first book at twelve. Work in Kids church at thirteen. Preach your first sermon at sixteen in Student Ministry. Serve EVERY-WHERE YOU CAN IN YOUR LOCAL CHURCH THIS SUNDAY. Become excellent at what God is calling you to do, week by week, yes to yes. Serving brings significance to your life.

DON'T GET CAUGHT UP IN THE FAME GAME

We so easily think we have not made a difference when our name (the brand of 'Me') is not spread across the internet. I must ask you, sweet girl, what are you DOING to develop yourself today? Are you serving in your kid's ministry at church? How about your local old-folks home? Operation Shoe Box? Mission trip? What about the babies in the nursery? Have you fed the homeless? Cleaned God's house? Everything I just listed, I did before the age of fifteen. (Operation Shoe Box had not begun, but we were already doing the same concept for Mexico, two times a year.)

FRONTLINE GIRLS get BUSY for Jesus, before the boyfriend, the husband, and the kids come along. Become useful for your Master NOW. Age never stops the FRONTLINE GIRL. She begins right where she is and says yes to her Master Jesus to serve Him with her whole heart.

It's your moment NOW to arise and sense the challenge like never before, to step up, big and bold, and SERVE your Master Jesus Christ. You are a FRONTLINE WOMAN.

You are a FRONTLINE GIRL... You are NO LONGER known for who you WERE, but you are now known for who you ARE. You are a member of the COMPANY OF JESUS.

You are no longer the diseased, rejected, eating-disorder girl, or the depressed, failure, fearful, addicted lady, but rather you are the CHOSEN beautiful whole-soul woman who has EVERY-

THING she needs to take her place on the FRONTLINE.

"Everything in the world is about to be wrapped up, so take nothing for granted. Stay wide-awake in prayer. Most of all, love each other as if your life depended on it. Love makes up for practically anything. Be quick to give a meal to the hungry, a bed to the homeless—cheerfully. Be generous with the different things God gave you, passing them around so all get in on it: if words, let it be God's words; if help, let it be God's hearty help. That way, God's bright presence will be evident in everything through Jesus, and he'll get all the credit as the One mighty in everything—encores to the end of time. Oh, yes!"

1 Peter 4:10-11 (MSG)

FRONTLINE DISCUSSION

What woman of the Bible speaks most to you about your life?

Why?

What attack, failure or heartbreak have you seen God strengthened you in, to minister to others with?

Pick out a partner and if you know her, be bold and tell her what greatness you see in her. What do you see her doing to serve her Master? What gifts do you see in her? What does her personality reflect for God's use? If you don't know her well, ask the Holy Spirit to show you something to encourage her in her FRONTLINE life.

What scripture do you feel God is speaking to you to strengthen your life right now? Find it and write it out.

FRONTLINE PRAYER

"Thank you, God, for using EVERYTHING in my life to serve and bless others. I ask that you take my tough times and reveal the strength you built within me. You are continually making an amazing ministry within me to serve the world with. I ask you to help me rise up now and take my place with confidence on the FRONTLINE. I'm not separate from what I do, to who I am in You—

"I AM ALL IN. All of me!" Here I am Master, use me in... Amen!"

FRONTLINE CONFESSION

Tough times are never an indication that my life is weak, but they're a sign of how strong I am in Jesus Christ. I will serve Him even more in my times of heartache and challenge. I persistently forge ahead and face what comes my way. I don't shrink back, but I pursue God's greatness in my life! I will NEVER quit or back down. I am a FOREVER FRONTLINE WOMAN.

SCRIPTURES TO BUILD YOUR FAITH

Isaiah 6:8; 1 Peter 5:7

Hebrews 10:39; Philippians 4:13

Hebrews 4:14; Ephesians 6:1

Chapter Four

DISCOVER YOUR MESSAGE

"My Sheep hear My voice."

John 10:27 (NIV)

YOUR MASTER'S VOICE IS NOW CLEARER THAN EVER.

You are distinguishing His voice even in this loud crazy world of pain, disruption, and injustice.

FRONTLINE WOMEN discover their unique personal message to the world by understanding the Master's true heart and how He wants to LOVE through her. She lets her preconceived opinions and judgments go as she embraces her Master's.

Let's listen with Love.... Open your heart... Express your message...

CONVERSATIONS WITH YOUR MASTER

There's an outcast at school. She smells odd, has undone hair and is tortured with words and rejection.

> *"Would you encourage her for Me? I'm standing at her heart's door knocking, but no one is bringing her to open the door. She needs your friendship."*

A guy with special needs who talks funny and wears thick glasses with big worn out tennis shoes. He's fumbling to carry his food tray.

> *"Quick, can you grab his tray and help him?"*

A little neighbor girl who has a sad life knocks on your door to play with the kids, and I'm just too busy to let her into my life. My makeup isn't on, and my home is a mess, so I send her away. Again.

> *"Today is her worst day yet. Her home is in turmoil, and she needs to see Me in a house with love, please invite her in."*

How many times does the church have to advertise the desperately needed help in kids church? I'm just SO busy, even though it's one time a month

and the prep-time is 20 minutes. Church kids
don't need me, so I look down at my phone.

> *"My House needs to radiate love, wrapped up in fun*
> *for My kids. They desperately need the unique love*
> *that only you can bring, just one time a month."*

There's that guy behind the cosmetic counter,
ughhhh, he's more beautiful than I am with his
perfect makeup, thick fashion lashes, nail polish,
and he's fluttering around loudly... did he stuff a
bra??

> *"He's My son. You have no idea what's brought him*
> *to this point in his life. Give him value. Please don't*
> *look down on him but look at him, right in the eyes.*
> *I love him as much as I love you, you're both my*
> *children. He's craving real genuine love... My love."*

There's a 'not so cool' mom who stands and looks
at me talking with all my flawless friends. I
wonder if I should include her. Oh right, she
wouldn't fit in. So, we turn sideways to block her
view into our world.

> *"She's ready to give up. She looks at you and thinks*
> *you have it all together, and everything you could*
> *ever want with your big cars, cute clothes, and*

flawless face. Please, just look at her and smile. Do you even know her name? She's been standing there, staring into your world since fall, and it's Easter."

Upload another selfie post. No content or substance. Just another brag. Another hit of dopamine. And that gorgeous girl, who I'm jealous of? Well, I'm passing on her picture because it stings and I'm not giving her another *flipping* like.

"Can you use your beauty for Me? If it became about Me, your jealousy would melt away, and your self-esteem would soar, and I would entrust you with even more."

I heard about Christian parents and their children being persecuted in other countries. I forgot to look up what I might be able to do.... ugh, probably not much.

"Heaven is filling up every single day with persecuted Christians. I need you to strengthen those yet to come with your prayers and love. I will direct you to more if you ask Me."

A friend bumps into me at the store, and she's telling me she's just been diagnosed with cancer, and more test are needed. I hug her and tell her I'll pray for her.

> *"Pray for her right now here in the store. It will strengthen her faith and relieve the burden she's deeply caring. She needs to know she's not alone. I'm with her, and I put you right in her path."*

Society is taking God out of everything everywhere. Oh well, I guess that's just how it is.

> *"No one can stamp My name out. Not with women like you spreading My love across the earth. Never give up or give in. YOU are on My Frontline."*

Pray before meals in public? Do people still even do that?

> *"Every time someone sees My people pray they think of Me. It's a seed, and I use everything."*

I see the ad for foster kids on television, and it hits my heart... again and again. Two years later... again.

> *"My little broken-hearted children need you. There are so many who are desperately waiting. Just waiting and asking Me for a family."*

I see the pregnant girl behind me is placing a couple food items on the cash register table. She's not dressed nice, and she's all alone. I better look straight ahead.

> *"I made sure you had that extra 20 dollar bill just for her today. She's been talking to Me about her needs all day. Please, just turn around and hand it to her."*

Volunteer at the old folk's home? It smells there.

> *"One visit with My forgotten elders, and you'd be forever changed. What's a little smell in the light of my glory and grace?"*

Giving. Why does my church always talk about money? I give my bit. They must make a fortune around here with as much as it's mentioned.

> *"You don't give to a building, a bill or a project. You give to Me. I've given you everything you have, and I don't need your bit, I need your all, your whole heart. As you give to Me, generosity will explode in your life and you'll receive the request with anticipation rather than dread. I love you and I enjoy blessing you!"*

Frontline Woman

That little bird looks hungry.

> *"It is. The snow has kept it from getting food.*
> *Why don't you throw out a little seed?*
> *A little special gift from Me."*

The safe house needs pajamas. Oh, I could get all my girlfriends to start collecting jammies.... yep, I sure could.

> *"Will you? It would bring so much happiness and*
> *support to My weary workers. They are tired and*
> *carry such a heavy burden. Just wait until you*
> *see their faces when you walk in with*
> *all those night clothes."*

Yikes, there's one of those ladies with a black Burka on. "God, I hope she doesn't blow this place up." I didn't say it out loud, but I bet my face did.

> *"She's so much more afraid than you are. Her life is*
> *not like yours. She drives by My houses of worship*
> *and wonders why you all are so loving to*
> *one another and she's waiting, just waiting for*
> *someone to show her My love. Smile at her*
> *and say a kind hello."*

I feel like God is telling me to walk over and tell that person He loves them and it's all going to be okay. I don't even know them. Better not.

"Oh, please don't hold back, they are at the end of themselves and I need them to know I'm right with them working things out, but they won't see My hand in it all for a while. Be bold."

Human Trafficking causes a lump in my throat.

"Don't be overwhelmed by the vast challenge. Just focus on the one. You can love the one! You can help one organization and make a massive difference."

I just keep thinking about them and I don't know why.

"I'm asking you to reach out to them. Invite them, AGAIN. Don't give up on them. I never gave up on you. They need to hear from you, from Me."

Teens these days... look at how they dress and act, it's such an embarrassment. Do they ever look up from their devices? I feel sorry for the future.

"I need you to invade the space of the teens in your world by reaching out to them with My unconditional love. Spend time with them and let

them see Me in you. Every woman should have the hand of an older woman and the hand of a younger woman, being mentored and mentoring."

They went to jail. They deserve everything they get!

"My child didn't start out a criminal. Life pulled them in that dark direction. Would you visit them? Reach out to them. They need my love too."

My in-laws are crazy! They make me so mad. They do everything opposite to me. I don't get them, and I hate being around them.

"My precious daughter, you must not compare; simply accept. When you love them, you love Me. See Me in their presence and choose contentment. There is so much peace in unity, and happiness in compassion."

That nurse looks exhausted, poor thing.

"She is so tired. She comforts My sick and fights disease all day long. Would you stop and smile at her? Tell her you appreciate all she does."

Just let that stupid tree die, who cares about it anyway?

"I do. It's My creation, and I gave you dominion
over it. If you don't want My vegetation, please
remove it with respect. Everything I created
works together."

They make me so angry!   How could they
say that about me? How can they do this to me?

"My dear girl, it has so little to do with you.
Can't you see into their personal pain?
They are living out of their hurt.
Can you love them unconditionally because
I love you unconditionally?
You know Me, so show Me to them."

The Pastor asked me to be one of the people to go
and pray for those who respond at altar time. I
don't know how to do that. I'm too scared.

"My shepherd would not ask you to do something he
didn't think you could do. All you need to do is speak
My love to each person. Just step out. I'll be
with you and you'll be so blessed."

What? They're addicted to prescription
drugs? No wonder they act so out-of-it all the
time! We're not hanging out with them anymore,
I knew something odd was up!

Frontline Woman

"Please don't push them out of your world. They need you now more than ever. Go right to them and have the tough conversation of how you can help and support. Tell them you love them regardless of how hard this will be and that you will be there with them each step of the way."

I've lived out almost every single one of the above scenarios and you have too.

We just aren't able to live the average life. FRONTLINE WOMEN are challenged to a higher place of entrustment, responsibility, and influence at ALL times.

There's little contentment in us when we don't respond to the voice of our Master Jesus Christ. When we hear His voice, a burning desire to obey Him consumes us.

Our capacity grows in the everyday small responses to His requests. This develops us for the BIG YES that takes us on world-changing adventures.

Get good at the daily easy things and watch the miraculous unfold in your life, shaping you, and conditioning you for more of the Master's use.

Please don't think, "Gosh, who has time for all of this?" This is not adding more to you... IT BECOMES YOU. It takes seconds to respond to God's voice and a minute or two to act... occasionally a little more.

You no longer live for yourself but now you live your life for the Master's use.

Open and willing. Sometimes it feels awkward and uncomfortable, but the payoff far exceeds the cost of living in the Master's company....

That's exactly what Jesus did. He didn't make it easy for himself by avoiding people's troubles but waded right in and helped out. "I took on the troubles of the troubled," is the way Scripture puts it. Even if it was written in Scripture long ago, you can be sure it's written for us. God wants the combination of his steady, constant calling and warm, personal counsel in Scripture to come to characterize us, keeping us alert for whatever he will do next.

May our dependably steady and warmly personal God develop maturity in you so that you get along with each other as well as Jesus gets along with us all. Then we'll be a choir—not our voices only, but our very lives singing in harmony in a stunning anthem to the God and Father of our Master Jesus!

Romans 15:3-6 (MSG)

FRONTLINE WOMEN are consistently developing their ability to hear our Master Jesus's voice. Look around with your eyes wide open and practice seeing needs, they are everywhere. Listen to your Master, He will speak and tell you what to do.

Don't be surprised if you end up being the woman who stands in front of the bathroom stall and is needed to help the handicap lady navigate the door. Don't turn away, help her! Help the struggling mom, the friend with homework, your sister's craziness, the tired teacher, your boyfriend's mom, the neighbor, your Pastor's wife, the person who fell.... STEP UP! God will continually place you where He needs you to be.

FRONTLINE DISCUSSION

After reading this Chapter did your perspective shift on anything? If so what?

If it's been easy to say yes to your Master, when was your last yes? What happened?

In the above scripture (Romans 15) toward the end, it talks about 'our very lives singing in harmony in a stunning anthem to God and Father of our Master Jesus.' Do you recognize and see the vast company of believers who are also traveling in the company WITH YOU? Who in your company has God placed in your heart?

Pray for them right now and consider a quick text, message, or call to encourage them in their FRONTLINE mission. Warriors get weary and we need the continued encouragement of one another.

Group Assignment: Take a partner this week and text each other quick mentions of your YES moments. Then shoot encouragement back. The power in joining together brings stronger momentum and deeply enriches friendship. No one is created to war alone on the FRONTLINE.

As your group wraps up, take hands with your partner and pray for divine appointments this week. Learning to listen takes time and soon your response will become natural.

FRONTLINE PRAYER

"Dear Jesus, help me to capture Your heart and see through Your eyes of unconditional love to everyone. Take all judgmental and religious attitudes from me. Just as You prayed to Your Father not to take me out of the world but to protect me while I'm here. I know You are with me every step. I partner with You to minister through me. Help me most with... In Your Name Amen."

FRONTLINE CONFESSION

'I listen to my Master's voice and I know it well. I've learned His ways and I'm alert to His direction. Unconditional love flows from me and I give it freely to everyone! I respond in grace with an open hand to everyone. Fear does not control me, and I rise up as a strong capable fearless FRONTLINE WOMAN.'

SCRIPTURES TO BUILD YOUR FAITH

John 8:3-12; Luke 7:36-50

John 4:1-30; 1 Corinthians 13:13

Luke 19:1-10; 1 John 3:16-18

Discover Your Message

Chapter Five

DEVELOP YOUR MESSAGE

You are fast becoming a DANGEROUS FORCE for your Master's use as you've said YES to the higher place of trust, responsibility and influence. You may think your life is on the quiet side but your Master Jesus is slowly amplifying your life and you're going places you may never have dreamed possible and I'm telling you, you will win battles that shift eternity forever!

Your own personal message begins in rock-hard form and develops unbelievable strength through the many pressures applied to your life.

Only through intense pressure, does a rock become a stunning diamond.

In my senior year I went through a program of half-day in high school, and the other half of the day

I left to go clock into Beauty College. I was so excited and my first day I showed up all cute in my new white uniform from head to toe, accessorized by a bright pink sweater and matching pink flower combs in my hair. It was the 80s, and I was really looking forward to getting my cosmetology license so I could have income doing hair while continuing to travel on the side with my puppets as that yielded very little money in those days.

Upon arriving to beauty school, all glammed up and ready to take on my new career, I looked out the window and a huge yellow school bus pulled up with LONG BEACH SCHOOL DISTRICT written on the side. Out popped student after student, in their white uniforms too, and I thought, "Wow, what fun is this gonna be!" I turned to the one other student from another local school who was all glammed up too and said, "Wow, Darla, this is going to be the best time ever!"

As it turned out, the new arrivals were all from a high school in downtown Long Beach where metal detectors and lockdowns were how you got in and out of school. I was only one student from a High School in Cerritos and my new friend Darla was from Lakewood where we did not need metal detectors or lockdowns in our school. I was a kind-hearted Jesus-Girl and Darla was a beautiful street-savvy girl, and I just have to say it, "We were sheep for the slaughter"... and particularly, THEY UTTERLY HATED, ME!

I was singled out as the church-girl from the other side of the tracks and these girls were BRUTAL. I decided I wasn't backing down from standing up for my Savior and it caused me to RISE UP courageously, regardless of the danger I personally faced.

Dangerous times made me DANGEROUS in my faith. I decided to stay as loving as I could under the circumstances and that ticked them off all the more. I had a hair-roller box slammed into the back of my head, pushing my face into a pay phone. There was almost daily sabotaging of my hair station, horrible embarrassing pranks; evil things were said to me ALL-THE-TIME and I don't think I ever saw the break room once. I was seriously afraid I would never come out. Thank God the bathroom was a single room because I'd of driven home before ever giving that a chance.

As you might imagine... I WAS SCARED ALL-THE-TIME. I wanted to QUIT every-single-day and then I'd hear a quote like the one by Maya Angelou, "Courage is fear that has said its prayers." I'd see a scripture, "Be joyful in hope, patient in affliction, faithful in prayer" Romans 12:12... I'd think of Queen Esther, "Maybe I was put here for such a time as this to love these girls to Jesus," so I'd stay yet another day, over and over again.

One afternoon we were all crowded in a smaller room practicing rolling perm rods on doll heads when a pretty bad earthquake hit and the students were all totally FREAKING OUT. I stepped into the middle of the room and calmed them all down, there were about 25 of us. The girls had so much fear and come to think of it; I did too, so I prayed a calm prayer out loud and they all settled down. For a moment, I saw they all 'got' me and they became much kinder, but it only lasted a few days.

We had a daily theory class and on a particular day one of the ringleaders, Emma walked up and with force, push-kicked the back of my plastic chair, slamming my whole body forward and they all burst into laughter.

I think she expected me to just take it but I stood up, turned towards her and said, "Wow, Emma, that was sooooo classy... You must feel really awesome with yourself."

It MAJORLY ticked her off!!

She hatefully reached into her mouth and (at this point I thought nothing could shock me) pulled out a large wad of her chewed up gum and flung it at my face. With my eyes wide open in disbelief, the gum came flying and as I tried to dodge it; it pinged my cheek and landed in my hair.

I instantly pulled her disgusting pre-chewed up white gum out of my hair-sprayed, feathered-back blonde hair, and threw it right back at her as she went to sit down. It skimmed the top of her hair-sprayed, feathered-back brunet head and I said, "I don't want your gross gum, Emma. You keep it... in YOUR mouth." Just then the instructor walked in and everything settled but you could sooo feel the tension in the room for the entire lesson.

Whew... I had stood up for myself and I knew it wasn't going to end well. I sat and prayed through the class, my cheeks were hot and my heart was pumping fast.

It was finally break-time so Darla and I got out quick and walked to the mall that our school was next to. Just as I walked in, all of a sudden someone grabbed a chunk of my hair from behind me. They were slinging me around, kicking me, slapping my face and then I felt a big punch on my other cheek—OMGosh...

It was Emma, and she was actually jumping me in the mall. My dear friend Darla started smacking her and grabbed a chunk of her hair, giving me a chance to spin myself painfully out of the grip she had on me, and I ran right into a men's shoe store. I frantically grabbed a shoe and held it up as the worker guys came to see what was going on.

My head was burning where my hair was just ripped out, my cheeks were on fire from being slapped and socked, and there I stood in a shoe store with a big man's shoe in my hand as Emma swayed back and forth just outside of the entrance.

She yelled at me at the top of her lungs, "I HATE YOU. I HATE YOUR GUTS!"

I answered her, "Emma, I love you!"

Ummm... I seriously have absolutely NO idea where 'I love you' came from, it just popped out from deep inside myself.

Somehow I yelled back love to her... God's love for her, and it shocked me, but it actually sounded right. I fully believe God's presence surrounded the moment. When God moves, often what you think would be weird and make no sense, actually comes out right and does what He wants it to do.

Standing there with the shoe in my hand, as calmly as I could I said, "Emma, why do you hate me so much when all I've ever done is to be is nice to you, and I'll never stop being nice to you ever?"

When she saw the security guards coming towards us she yelled, "I SO HATE YOU CINDY" and she vanished. I turned to thank everyone as the security guards said, "Is everything good here?"

I said, "I think so", and then Darla grabbed me and we ran back to school as fast as we could. I was shaking like a leaf with hot tears streaming down my burning slapped, socked cheeks. Emma didn't return to the school that afternoon, I think she knew she'd crossed the line.

The next afternoon I was called into the beauty school's office and the head instructor kindly said, "We were informed about the incident in the mall yesterday and for your safety and protection we are sending you to another school. These girls are out of control and we don't know what to do with them. We are deeply concerned for your security. You need to go now, today. I called Ms. Kay at American Beauty College about you and your situation and she's agreed to take you regardless of the program you are in. Go pack up now and go straight there."

I went right out and packed up my hair station. I was relieved and a little excited but also quite sad as I felt like all the crap I just went through was for nothing.

Surprisingly, I was shocked at how many girls turned lovely and came out of the woodworks and grabbed me and told me how sorry they were for being horrible and never standing up for me. Several said that they too loved Jesus but didn't want all the trouble.

WHY DID THESE GIRLS STAND BACK and let one of their own suffer alone? This crushed me on one hand, but at least I stood strong for my Savior, and I decided that was all that truly mattered. I hugged Darla goodbye, and I was gone.

THIS CALL IS FOR THE GIRL WHO COULD CARE LESS ABOUT THE DANGER... THEY-ARE-THE-DANGER!

They CHOOSE the higher call.

I showed up to my new Cosmetology School, "American School Of Beauty" which incredibly, backed onto the property of the church I attended. I had originally chosen the other school because it was right by my home but I felt so much comfort and peace seeing my precious, "LORDS CHURCH" right next door and slowly I relaxed.

One afternoon I was doing my classroom theory time, learning about scalp diseases when two new students walked in. I looked up only to see this punker chick who hated me from high school standing there with another girl. Nooooo! That was it, here we go again! I was heartbroken.

───────◦───────

OK... So here's the deal. I've always LOVED all things in the beauty world. Don't forget I had been on platforms since I was a little kid. I was a VERY beautiful girl... 'ONLY BECAUSE I KNEW HOW TO CREATE BEAUTY!'

Long before the beauty bloggers I was contouring, adding gorgeous lashes, lining my lips, and dressing in top 80s styles and I often intimidated other girls. Now mix that with me being a stand up girl for God and loving pretty much everyone. I was often hated. I knew I just had to do my time as a teenager and I'd be free from all the nonsense. So I tried to stay loving and kind, and I KNEW my calling was much higher than what I so often endured, it was NOT easy. FRONTLINE GIRLS learn to BE themselves.

"Do not be conformed to this world!"

Romans 12:2 (NIV)

Just be you! Whoever you are, be it full on.

So now there stood another enemy in my new school with punked-out hair, safety pins in weird places and real tats—who had tattoos in high school!? Back then, no one... but her! And I thought, "This is it—now for sure, I'm dead!"

We locked eyes, and I looked away and my heart beat frantically. It was like light and darkness colliding.

After class, she walked right up and stood over me. I slowly looked up into her eyes and I was ready for the start of another horrible season...

She had regularly walked by me in High School and would point her two fingers towards my eyes and go, 'SSSSSSSS" like a snake. Yeah, she pretty much freaked me out, and now I was face to face with one of the scariest chicks I knew... Everyone talked about her and respected her wild craziness!

She simply introduced herself and said, "Ha-ha, I know I'm scary but really I'm cool. I've seen you at school and I think I scared you a few times—Sorry about that." I was speechless... what do you say to that? Nothing. I just smiled. Then I stood up and out of the blue I said, "Come on, I'll show you around."

Through it all we fell in friendship-love with each other. I loved her in all her sin-craziness and she loved me in all my holy-craziness. She kindly taught me the ways of the world and I lovingly taught her the ways of Jesus.

We had so many laughs and beauty school adventures, then one day I was standing doing a perm on a little sweet old lady, and as I looked up into the mirror... I blinked twice and looked at the reflection again... No, you've got to be kidding me.... It was real. It was Emma, looking right at me. She and her friend were standing in their white uniforms. They had become students there, and my heart dropped to the floor.

I was a bit tougher now, more dangerous. God was quickly developing me and I was learning the hurt of the world in a whole new way... No one is born evil. No precious kindergartner raises her hand and says "Teacher, when I grow up I wanna be hateful, bitter, mean, etc." She has hopes and dreams. She wants to love and be loved. Deep inside, she's created to live for her Savior.

I dismissed myself and went to find my friend. She assured me, "Don't you worry about a thing. I'll take care of you. She won't dare hurt you. Not this time."

Later the next day, my punker friend came up to me and said, "Come on, Emma wants to talk to you."

She grabbed my arm and walked me to the front door. I took a deep breath, "As long as you come too I'm fine so don't leave me." We both stepped outside.

There sat Emma and her friend on the window ledge of the school. Emma took a long drag on her cigarette and as she blew the smoke out she looked up at me with one squinted eye. She looked horrible, wrecked, sad, older.

"Thanks for coming out here." I stayed quiet. She took another drag of her smoke. "I haven't had your kind of life Cindy. I've had a shi_ _y life. You see my lip?" (Her bottom lip had a big bubble on it that had been there since the day I met her. I remember really noticing it when she ripped her gum out of her mouth.)

"Well, my step-dad pounded me and its permanent." She then shared a few more very sad hurtful personal things and said, "What all I did to you back at the other school was effed up and I don't even know why I did it." Suddenly her friend stood up and I got an even closer look at Emma. She had tears in her eyes as she took another big drag and stood up. As she blew her smoke out to the side

I stepped over to her and I reached out and I hugged her. I had tears in my eyes too.

I don't want to sound like a saint, I'M NOT! I'm just a girl who said yes to my Master Jesus, and I meant it full-heartedly. He was developing within me a rise to the FRONTLINE of entrustment. He had bigger plans for me. He was developing a fearless heart. He was allowing the heat to refine me. He was developing my voice... My message.

As I hugged Emma, she was stiff but I could tell she received it. "It's all in the past now. Let's let it go and start over."

Over it was. I decided to always say a kind "Hi" to her, as she did to me. I'd even sit with her occasionally and check up on her and tell her I'd pray for her.

You have to LOVE someone when they LEAST deserve it because that's when they most desperately need it. Please read that again... and I must tell you, this is your most treasured gift— Love people for WHO they are, not what they DO.

Finally, the day came when I had completed enough hours to clock out of beauty school for the very last time. All the students gather around and together you count the seconds until your moment arrives to clock out...

I slid my card in and BOOM, 1,600 hours were completed!! Everyone cheered me on! After all the craziness, I had actually made it. I was now a fully trained hairdresser ready for the state test!

I looked over and there was Emma clapping with everyone... My past enemy, clapping. The girl who made my life hell and beat (what felt like) the tar out of me at one time, but not today. Today she was my friend.

As her time came to hug me, it was heartfelt, and she said, "God, Cindy (big hug) Chick, I'm sooo gonna miss you." It was surreal, and a moment you never forget. It's when your Master smiles and your message gets embedded in who you are, and the enemy can NEVER SHUT YOU UP AGAIN— Never.

God can do anything, you know—far more than you could ever imagine or guess or request in your wildest dreams! He does it not by pushing us around but by working within us, his Spirit deeply and gently within us.

Ephesians 3:20-21 (MSG)

A couple years passed, and I was at my church when a slightly familiar girl walked up and said, "You're Cindy, right? Do you remember me from beauty school?"

In my mind I said, "Uhhhhh... yeah! I remember you... bully, hateful, loud, rude, laughed at me." Then she interrupted my thoughts, "I have prayed so many times to see you and I can't believe you are standing here."

She reached out and took my hand, "PLEASE forgive me for how I treated you. I swear, I couldn't sleep at night for how awful I was... So, I met this guy, and he took me to church and I found God, Cindy, I found God—Can you believe it? I've been asking Him to help me find you so I could tell you! Can you forgive me? I'm so, so sorry and I just wanted you to know.... Oh, and remember so and so, well... She found God too!"

I had often thought my time was a waste in my first beauty school. I'd think, "Well, maybe God used it all to make me strong." Which was true... God had used all this to develop the brave girl He had placed inside me, but then my mind would wander back only to what I could see...

It seemed like nothing much came of trying to lead those girls to Jesus... But as you know my FRONTLINE Friend... God's love is like wildfire and once someone catches just the flicker of it, nothing can put the flames out and it'll spread into every area of life. I simply lit flickers of love into their hearts and He took care of the rest.

Sharing His love is NEVER wasted and everything is working towards His plan. We are His messengers of love developed to shine brightly for our Master's use whenever, wherever, and to whoever.

By this, all men and women will know that you are My disciples (FRONTLINE WOMEN) when you LOVE one another.

John 13: 35 (NIV)

FRONTLINE DISCUSSION

Have you ever stood up for your faith?

Were you afraid? What happened?

Looking back over your life, can you see how God was developing your message through a tough experience? What happened?

Have you ever loved someone in spite of their rejection of your faith? When?

FRONTLINE PRAYER

"I commit to being strong for you dear Lord Jesus! I ask that you help me to be courageous in my stand-up moments for You! Help me to never be ashamed of who You are in my life and I ask that You open doors for me to shout Your fame across the earth. I pray now, dear Lord, that You STRENGTHEN my heart and give my spirit courage to... Thank you Jesus, Amen."

FRONTLINE CONFESSION

I am bold, mighty and solid in my faith in Jesus Christ. I speak love and I am LOVE to everyone regardless of their distain or resentment of my Faith or of me. I don't back down from love ever! Perfect LOVE casts out ALL fear and I will love when I'm afraid. My God is my strength, my courage, and the power I draw from. Everything is possible with my God so no matter who may be against me I know my God is for me!

SCRIPTURES TO STRENGTHEN YOUR FAITH

Romans 1:16; Ephesians 4:1-32

Exodus 14:13; Matthew 22:37-39

Romans 8:38-39; Exodus 18:23

Develop Your Message

Chapter Six

DELIVER YOUR MESSAGE

YOU ARE GODS MESSAGE BRINGER SO RAISE YOUR VOICE AND BE HEARD!

Your voice may never ring out over a microphone or be delivered from a stage (maybe) but some of the most powerful messengers, with the most effective voices for the Master on the FRONTLINE, are women who are busy DOING their Father's business. We may never "HEAR" her, but her life laid down for the Master is RESOUNDING.

I think of my legendary friend, Leigh Ramsey, who founded the "SHE RESCUE Home" in Cambodia for rescuing girls from human trafficking and child prostitution. (sherescuehome.org)

I was invited on a trip to Cambodia for female Pastors by my brave Pastor friend Jillian Chambers (who I so honor!) She confidently led the way from America to an incredible overseas adventure.

After arriving and settling in, Jillian walked us girls down the street to a local restaurant to all meet up together for the first time. Just around the corner, there were several little children laying on tattered blankets with their mama to rest and ask for money.

There was a beautiful woman with a leopard headscarf wrapped around her long blonde tresses, bending down, picking up one of the babies. In her lovely Aussie accent I could hear she was doting and loving on the tiny baby and telling the mom how beautiful her baby was.

You could see strength in this woman right off, and sure enough, it was Leigh Ramsey, mother to many Cambodian children who have been rescued after being sold into human trafficking.

Frontline Woman

To say this woman is a legend is an understatement but it will have to do for now. She is a voice that gives direction to the world to stand up and make a difference.

The second most brilliant person in all of this is the one BEHIND Leigh and her name is Hilary Ramsay, Leigh's sister-in-law. This woman is one of the most effective FRONTLINE women you'll meet. She is tireless with consistent energy as she organizes, sets up, oversees, arranges, helps, and is KIND and LOVING all-the-time! You may never hear her voice, but you SEE her efforts and the effect of her FRONTLINE life right into eternity.

When we all met up and began talking, Hilary asked about my Melinda. Melinda is my brilliant behind-the-scenes FRONTLINE Woman.

Without her, I'd be totally ineffective. SHE HATES A MICROPHONE! But her message resounds through God's House in organizing, setting up, overseeing, arranging, and she stays kind and loving at all times. She has tried to retire a couple of times but the pull to her place on the Frontline does not diminish because of age.

Hilary had been conversing from Australia to my Melinda about the trip and the many details (and Melinda does not miss a detail.) As we all talked, we acknowledged that EACH ONE OF US HAD BRILLIANT FRONTLINE WOMEN BEHIND US! (When I ministered in Canada I had my precious Cheryl and let me tell you she never missed a thing, and she still is a FRONTLINE WOMAN to this day.) As I speak at all kinds of churches, I get to meet a vast amount of FRONTLINE organizers and they ROCK God's Houses! I think of Gail, Shelly, Annie, Toni, Cheryl, Patty, Stefanie, Brittney and I could go on and on!

We must NEVER belittle our stance on the FRONTLINE, thinking a stage or microphone is the most effective way to be heard. The message we have within us may be delivered in a powerful voice of expression in organizing, details, overseeing, setting up, cleaning up, administrating and forging ahead with great service. Often voices over the microphone are visionaries who can dream it up, impassion everyone to the cause, and then wonder how in the heck it's really going to happen, and it's FRONTLINE WOMEN and MEN that step up who MAKE IT A REALITY!

While getting ready to go to Cambodia we each were requested to bring certain things that were needed for the work there. I collected over 30 Barbies, placing each in their own zip-lock bag with outfits, shoes, little plastic animals, and tiny toys. I also brought 50 pounds of burlap that was delivered to my home and placed in my suitcases. It was an enormous endeavor. I was VERY nervous about everything but I just kept telling God I was His hands, heart, and feet, and He could use me any way He wanted, even if it was just to deliver all the goods I was bringing... God just smiled.

A few weeks before leaving, Hilary sent me a message "Hello LaCinda, We heard you were a hairdresser and the girls at our home need haircuts, can you bring your supplies and cut hair?" I was ecstatic... I cried as I can't tell you HOW MANY TIMES I thought, "What can God do with me as a hairdresser?"

God just laughs and says, "Watch Me."

Then I received another message, "Hello LaCinda, will you be doing your puppets? The kids would love you to bring your puppets. We have an interpreter for you and he will travel with you, out to the villages."

I decided if God wanted to use my crazy talent of throwing my voice and not moving my lips, then I would find the biggest most adorable lightweight puppet I could.

We found a big fluffy lavender furry ball of fun and we named her, "LOVIE." We decked her out in jewels and a bow. I just knew I had to learn a song in the native Cambodian language.

My older son Stetson is a brilliant researcher, and he found out the language they spoke was Khmer. He then realized there are little to no Christian words in the Khmer language that fit the song I wanted to sing. He could only help me with a few words. To make a short story of a long journey, I ended up meeting a Cambodian on the plane and he sang as much as he could into my phone as I recorded, but even he didn't know the words I needed.

No one had a Khmer word for Jesus until I walked into a coffee shop. We stopped on the way to our first village outing, where Lovie was to be one of the guests, but our song was not ready yet, and I wasn't about to give up hope.

A group of young men who worked there was standing around the coffee counter looking at all us pretty Pastor girls, so I broke the awkward moment and said in a loud voice, "ខ្ញុំរីករាយណាស់" meaning, "I'M SO HAPPY" in Khmer, and they all got SO happy too!

I tried to sing my song to them when a sweet young man came right over and said in his broken English.... "I know what you try to say and you say wrong! Come here and I show you." He walked me away from everyone and said, *"When I was boy I was help by God people and they save me from very bad life. You say song like this..."*

You see, little boys are sold in Cambodia and raised to be "lady-boys" as they are called. The boys are sold and prostituted in devastating ways. I could tell he had been one of these young precious guys who was in the process of restoration from a very hard life. Human trafficking is not just a female injustice. It's vile evil upon humanity for one reason. Money.

My new-found friend coached me and worked with me as he sang into my phone and after a big hug and blessings, off we went as I practiced over and over on our drive to the village in the tuck-tuck.

When we arrived at the village, the little kids came pouring out. There were so many sad deformities and even open sores on some, but they had bright eyes and were full of hope that we had come to visit them. Pastor Charla Turner told a mesmerizing story of Jesus with pictures and the kids just took it all in. It was then Lovie's turn to sing, and out it came. You should have seen the kid's faces light up when this big furry purple puppet sang in their language.

Remember, these kids live deep in a little village or out on tall planks over the ocean, and they don't have TV or the internet. No electricity, running water or basic things we take for granted.

We had given the children little airplanes to build, and they did not even know that they were supposed to fly. Several needed help to understand a tootsie pop sucker, and then this big adorable eyed puppet pops out and sang to them. It was one of my finest FRONTLINE moments.

No microphone! No stage! No fame! No internet to splash my picture across my friend's screens. Just us Pastor girls in a company of women traveling from village to village. Town to town, taking the message of love to sweet, very needy precious people.

GOD IS SO GOOD TO HIS FRONTLINE WOMEN

You can imagine how demanding running a huge endeavor like SHE Rescue Home would be with over thirty girls, multiple teachers, leaders, and everyone it takes to fight injustice in a country so overtaken with child sex trafficking. Leigh was exhausted in her heart because when you fight such a revolting injustice the pressure is massive and at times tough to bear.

Each month the budget is substantial and must be met by donations. The girls and leaders have serious needs, sicknesses, emotional scarring, and so much that must be overseen. This all takes incredible steady faith and determination.

Leigh had been asking God for a sign that she was making a difference. We all could see the MASSIVE influence and difference she was making, but she needed to see it up close and personal, she needed a message from her Master.

Her sign came straight from heaven. On the night we all arrived and met for dinner, a call came that there was a first-of-its-kind rescue. I can't share any details or much about a lot of things to protect our girls but I can tell you a brothel was busted and her home received several girls, and one was expecting a baby very soon. It SO blessed us to see her so encouraged as God was saying, "I'm with you every step and my FRONTLINE WOMAN is making a HUGE impact."

Once again, FRONTLINE WOMEN understand the weight of the FRONTLINE. It is not an easy fight, but it's oh-so-sweet to win and gain ground.

I just happened to get in on a little of this amazing win. It was haircut day and each little girl would take her turn under the water spicket to wet her dark hair and then she'd hop up on a chair to have her hair cut in her desired style. It was so cute as our interpreter relayed what they each wanted.

After well over twenty haircuts in the hot sticky heat, a slight disturbance happened with the house mums and my interpreter. It turned out the newly rescued girls wanted cuts too, but they were mean, abused, and disrupted in life. I said, "Oh, I don't care, just bring them to me."

One by one these young girls (no more than fourteen or fifteen years old) sat in my chair and I had a chance to just love on them.

My first girl's hair was very burnt from harsh hair-coloring so I found two small bottles of conditioner and because she knew a little english, I directed her how to use it. But when I blinked the conditioner disappeared. She and I made eye contact, and she showed me how she had hid it from the other girls and she whispered: "They take away." Then she put her finger to her lip for me to be quiet. She was so lovely, but the minute the other girls came in, her demure completely changed.

As I lifted each girl's hair up to cut it, their roots were almost fully grey. Why in the world would this be? And then I was told privately by my interpreter that starvation and abuse would have caused this.

Throughout the day, my interpreter wore a medical mask. I had wanted to ask her why she was wearing it so finally when all the haircuts were done, I looked straight at the mask she had on and said, "Why, beautiful girl, do you wear a mask?" She answered, "Oh, because I have no front teeth."

I knew why. It was the same reason the girl's hair had turned grey.

I told her, "I'm buying you a new smile." I have done this before for several women in my world who show up with no teeth. It's wrong when we can fix something as important as a smile. My sweet interpreter had her mask on because she didn't want the pretty American girls to see her broken smile. Sure enough, I went home and raised the money, and we got her new teeth. It wasn't long later, and we received pictures of her on her wedding day, smiling so utterly beautiful!

Once again. no microphone or stage—No fame or glory—Just a smile on a lovely girl's face.

YOUR MESSAGE

Isn't it awesome to hear about all that God can do through a FRONTLINE WOMAN out on the battlefield of injustice....

Yeah, it's really phenomenal...

But I want you to know how valuable YOUR MESSAGE IS TO YOUR WORLD!

Almost everyone I ask can remember the first time they heard the words "Human Trafficking".

Although it's been going on since the beginning of time, the church is becoming greatly aware of it. It's sickening, and when you come to understand it, you are never the same again.

The first time I heard the term "Human Trafficking" was from Sandie Morgan, Director of the Global Center for Women & Justice at Vanguard University. She was speaking so brilliantly at a conference I was attending, and then later during a break, I just *happened* to stand by her in the ladies' room (which was no accident) and we began talking. We made friends, and I eventually invited her to come to my church and conduct a Human Trafficking awareness training seminar.

In preparation for the seminar, we had ten beautifully packed, black with pink polka dotted, suitcases. They were each filled with necessities and all kinds of pretty things, ready to go at any time that our local ICE agent called with a human trafficking rescue. We were excited and ready to learn how to combat this ugliest of crimes.

Sandie Morgan lovingly smacked us all between the eyes when she challenged our paradigm of trying to help rescued victims, to PREVENTING Human Trafficking in the first place....

"You want to prevent Human Trafficking? I'll tell you exactly how to prevent it. Make your children's church amazing. Make your youth program over the top. Make your church radiant and relevant to the community. Please don't tell me you want to make a difference out there (as she pointed to the doors) when you are not making a difference in here!"

Somebody say, "Hashtag BOOM!" We were challenged right in the core of our hearts!

I can tell you some "Whoop-Glory" stories of the hustle it takes to make Cambodia rock awesome! I can share miraculous mission stories from foreign lands, but FRONTLINE WOMEN get busy in their own backyard! They stand up for justice right in their own churches, filled with HURTING PEOPLE!!

"Heaven is my throne and the earth is my footstool. What kind of a house will you build for me, says the lord!"

Acts 7:49 (NIV)

Just the other day I went into our own kid's church and there were kids standing and singing with sweet smiles across their cheeks, but deep inside many are brokenhearted. There stood siblings, heartbroken over a horrible divorce that their parents are in the middle of.

Another large family of kids was standing and worshiping, without mommy dressing them for church that day, because a doctor misjudged her pain while she sat in the ER. Needlessly, she fell to her early death as she sat waiting. Now there's no mommy at home, of 6 kids who are the most precious kids you'd ever meet.

I then look over and see another little family of brothers and sisters, dressed so nicely by their adopted parents, because their biological mommy has a drug issue, and daddy is in prison.

I go into the preschool room and a beautiful little girl grabbed my cheeks and said, "Did you know my mommy is dead?" Yes, her mommy had just died a sad death that week... and in the nursery two different babies, from totally different homes, are being raised by a family member, because one mommy is on drugs and the other mommy is mentally unstable...

On my way out, I get stopped by a tearful hug from two preteen kids saying goodbye because they are leaving to another state, because their custody just turned in that direction. This is not even the flood of prayer cards from the adults that come in with desperation written all over them!

I could go on and on, and this is in my own home church on just ONE Sunday. It's a beautiful church with amazing people, but people are people, and everyone hurts, and everyone bleeds, and EVERY FRONTLINE WOMAN IS CALLED TO ANSWER HER MASTER WITH WHAT SHE

IS DOING TO BUILD HIS HOUSE HERE ON EARTH. The House that God has entrusted to us... No microphone or stage needed. Do you have love? God has someone needing your love this Sunday.

Grandmas can rock babies in the nursery so tired mommies can enjoy a service and get stronger. I think of beautiful Sherry in my own church. She works full-time and has a full life of being a grandma, but she NEVER misses her commitment to her morning to love on the babies! It touches my heart as I look in and know what so many of our little babies are facing, and there she is, LOVING them right on the FRONTLINE for their little lives.

A tired mommy can show up during the week with her little ones and wipe toys down and clean up the nursery. I think of lovely Crystal, who's little boy was born really early. We were with them when the Doctor kindly told them to let their little preemie go to Heaven.

They rose up and said, "ABSOLUTELY NOT" and thank God they did, as he has grown into such a blessing! Mama and son, along with her other children, show up and clean the nursery and kids' buildings, as a blessing to God's kids. Her FRONTLINE place, alongside motherhood, is making God's home clean, fresh and fun.

PLEASE HEAR ME when I say, FRONTLINE girls, out of high school and into college, should absolutely serve a MINIMUM of one Sunday a month in Kid's ministry. You are young, and no one will have the kind of influence you have over the next generation. The kids want to be like you and the happiness you'll get when you hear, "HI TEACHER", with a big hug, is so worth it.

You'll even bump into your kids when you are outside of church and they will run up to you and love on you, making your entire day lovely! Don't hold back... "I'm so BUSY" with school, work or whatever...

Your love may be the VERY thing that spares a life of heartache with your beautiful YES to Jesus to simply love His kids.

If your church has more than one service, you can serve one and attend one.

Women ask me all the time, "How do I get to the place to be like you and go out and speak."

What they are really saying is, "How do I get to be on a stage and hold a microphone and speak?" I understand that desire and I always answer with the same question, "What do you have in you to speak about? What's your message? What do you do at home in your local church?"

Your message is loud and clear, in ACTION, WAY BEFORE YOU GET A MICROPHONE and a platform, and if God has graced a girl to have a MIC before it's earned it's not up to us to judge her. Her refining time will come, and part of it is having that MIC and platform a little too soon.

I've watched this more than once... Give her time. She'll rise up and take her place.

You keep focused on making a difference in your own world right now, in the House God has placed you in.

Don't be deceived into thinking you don't have time! You'll be robbed of the greatest adventure of your life! We all go through seasons of pulling back, and needing rest and refocusing, but don't let it last too long and steal from you your reward in Heaven.

I want to hold my head up high as I walk into heaven to meet my Master. I want to bravely answer Him, "Yes, Jesus, I did ALL unto You with my whole heart!"

I want my life to include "Loving what He loves". Oh, how I want Him to feel gratitude for something small I may have done to answer His question, "What kind of house did you build for me?"

I don't want to have filled my life with only busy-ness, more stuff and more of myself. I want my kingdom-life to have mattered, and the only way that will happen is standing on that FRONTLINE and DELIVERING THE MESSAGE GOD HAS PUT WITHIN MY HEART! I know you do too! We can, its simple... Serve His House.

FRONTLINE DISCUSSION

In my book, Creative Expression there is a discovery test to find and develop your God given expression.

(You can find it at lacindabloomfield.com)

Some of us are gifted in communicating and others are gifted in administrative areas or both.

What kind of message bringer are you?

How do you express your message?

What is a vocation, talent, hobby or gift you are considering using for God? Did you ever think, "How could God ever use this?"

I mentioned earlier in this chapter how I had packed 50 pounds of burlap to take to Cambodia. This is for enterprise... kingdom business.

The burlap is divided up, along with other material, and it's taken out to the girl's families to cut, sew, and stamp sayings on small beautiful pillows. The families also make beautiful bracelets out of yarn and twine.

The goal is to get their family financially stable and emotionally strong through their relationship with SHE Rescue Home. Many girls have been able to safely return to their family because of this enterprise.

Poverty is almost always the challenge and this brilliant enterprise helps restore the entire family.

Would you consider contacting SHE Rescue Home and selling their products at your next event, or giving some as gifts for your next party? (www.itsnotok.com)

Do you have any ideas for an enterprise you could do to fund the difference you want to make on the FRONTLINE?

I collected 30 Barbies as a teenager (I think it was 33 to be exact) to take to Mexico. This was not new to me. Orvella Philips, from the Lord's Church in Bellflower, CA, who is a mentor and forever LEGEND, has led teams to Mexico and Indian Reservations for YEARS and still does to this day.

Serving Jesus in Mexico at age 16, with my doll Tecla, and our dear Mexican Pastors

She took me, twice a year, with her to Mexico. I'd help lead the children's crusades with my ventriloquism doll Tecla during the day, and then she'd teach me to preach at night. (Just a small word but to me it was massive!) I noticed when we would offer prayer at the end of our services that SO many would ask us to pray for their hurting mouths. Then I realized they had zero dental hygiene. At 14 years old I began a toothbrush and toothpaste drive. We collected HUNDREDS of toothbrushes and toothpastes and took them to Mexico twice a year. I taught hygiene to the kids and how to take care of their mouths.

WHAT NEED DO YOU SEE THAT YOU CAN FILL?

Be brave and get the word out! Change a life. Contact your local mission, food bank, old folks' home, detention center, inner-city school, foster home advocate, adoptive services, teen home for pregnant moms, prison, group home, recovery home, and ask them what they need?

Do they need toilet paper, baby bottles, diapers, female supplies, books, gifts, pajamas, slippers, lip gloss, food, toys, school supplies, toiletries, hygiene items, home repair, blankets? I want to tell you, every single item I just mentioned, I have put a call out and we have supplied it. It is so much easier than you think! We have also collected what we called, "Purses With Purpose" where we gathered gently used handbags and filled them with toiletries, gum, and pretty things, and gave them to women in need.

Each year we host a Saturday morning called, "Beautiful You" where we give underprivileged women a Purses With Purpose handbag filled with essentials, a full outfit, and professional hairdressers and makeup artists do their hair and face, along with mani's, massages, and much more, to lift the lives of women who are hurting, all the while giving their kids an amazing time!

You can make a HUGE difference right where you are at today. No waiting for a microphone, thinking that's the big win—NO! The big win is in the day-to-day, small personal touches.

What can you do? Who can you include?

HOW TO APPROACH YOUR CHURCH

Make an appointment to see your outreach Pastor or leader. If you do not have one, find out who the proper person is to talk to.

1. Be prepared. Do not show up with a brilliant idea and expect THEM to do the work. Often leaders get stuck with someone else's vision and it's very discouraging. If you are called to the FRONTLINE, be prepared to do the work.

   Show up with your idea in a concise manner, with your questions written down, and write the answers so you don't forget (No more than5 questions). If you need more, come back later. Only stay 20 to 30 minutes, then dismiss yourself politely, thanking them for their time. Leave knowing your next step.

2. Always think TEAM. Who can help you? Who can be part of what you have in mind? Who can take ownership with you to accomplish more?

3. Think of creative ways to promote your cause. Chair-drops (nicely made and cut straight), a classy decorated box in the lobby for collection, letters to businesses, emails, etc. Do all this under the direction of the leader.

4. Consider storage. Where are you planning on storing all the stuff before distribution? (I had purses coming out of my ears! Toiletries were everywhere! Canned goods across the walls.) Storage is an issue. Just think it out so you are

prepared. If no storage exists, then take it home or find someone who can help store it all.

5. Make distribution day fun! Video it, take photos (leave the faces of those you're blessing out if necessary). Honor your Pastor or leader on that day. Send out thank-you messages to donors, and anyone who was a blessing to you.

6. Meet back up with your leader to thank them (It's a good idea to have actual photos printed of the giving day to show them) and get their feedback and ideas for the next event.

CONSIDERATION: is there no outreach/mission leader? FRONTLINE WOMEN STEP UP AND LEAD!

Ask the Pastor if there is a desire for someone to lead Outreach and if so, seriously consider taking it on... Slowly at first, with one event, by following the guidelines above... See what God will do.

FRONTLINE PRAYER

Precious Savior, help me to boldly raise my voice across the earth! Use me to light up the world that seems covered in darkness. I earnestly pray for my local church where the bruised and broken come into. Bless my Pastors and leaders with wisdom and endurance. Show me how I can support them and encourage them in all they do to lead Your people. Give me creativity and fresh ideas to make Your House radiant and attractive to the lost and our church family. Show me how we as a church can reach out into our community and the world. In your name Amen.

Take a moment to listen and write what God is speaking to you?

FRONTLINE CONFESSION

I LOVE my local church. I LOVE my Pastors and Leaders. I SERVE God's House and His people BOLDLY as I STEP UP TO THE FRONTLINE and raise my voice to be heard in the way God created me to serve Him. I take daily action to live life well, serving the purposes of God in my life. I commit to making God's House radiant to all who walk in.

I lay my life down to the purposes of my Master Jesus Christ. Here I am Lord, Show me! Use me! Send me!

SCRIPTURES TO STRENGTHEN YOUR FAITH

Isaiah 41:10; Philippians 2:3; John 3:30

Mark 10:42-45; 1 Timothy 1:12; Ephesians 6:11

Pastor Charla Turner and I sharing Jesus with Children in Cambodia

It's **NOT OK**

Human Trafficking Mission Trip for Female Pastors, SHE Rescue Home, Cambodia

Left to right: Charla Turner, LaCinda Bloomfield, Hilary Ramsey, Dana Adams, Jillian Chambers, Staci Capaldi, Leigh Ramsey—Founder of SHE Rescue, Lisa Marie Seaton, Jennifer DeWeerdt.

Chapter Seven

PURPOSED FOR MISSION

Your message is now developing rapidly and most likely you are experiencing strategic daily missions that God is placing you on.

Your Master has a great need for you and if not already, you will find yourself in odd places at surprising times. You may think you are having déjà-vu, and other times you will feel strongly that you must go a different way or stay longer. You will look at someone and offer something right out of the blue, and as you do it, you won't even care if they tell you no.

You are on your Master's mission and there is happily no turning back now. In fact, you have a BRING IT ON desire.

There are also VERY PURPOSEFUL missions where you plan, strategize, and go take God's love to the ends of the earth.

I strongly believe, and have seen over and over, the most effective foreign missions are attached to God's House. There are so many missions trips to go on, but in my experience, a consistent relationship with the missionaries/organizations is the most effective form of missions. These relationships keep the strongest through the local church.

Pastor Danielle Payment who is a dear-to-my-heart Pastor girl, who I've watched go from a youth leader to youth Pastor, and now she is the Outreach Pastor at her church (Capital Christian Center, Olympia, WA, Senior Pastor Dave Minton).

She also serves alongside Pastor Rick Warren in his P.E.A.C.E plan, and she is really doing phenomenal things in Africa.

Danielle had been taking people from their church to Africa for well over a year when I asked her, "Please take me!"

As we talked about it she said, "Oh, we are still building relationships with everyone there.

We are establishing trust and we are in no rush. So I want to take you when we begin our training." The results of this strategy are TRANS-FORMING.

You can look into the P.E.A.C.E. Plan through Saddleback church. What I LOVE about Pastor Rick's formula is that it's kept SIMPLE, and it's very EFFECTIVE. A trained P.E.A.C.E. church team goes into villages that are underdeveloped and builds relationships with local Pastors and leaders. Once trust is built, the P.E.A.C.E. church team trains the indigenous team to effectively lead their own people in building their village.

The building supplies are financially supported by the P.E.A.C.E. church, which is so exciting for everyone as they are part of creating this new village that is centered around God's House, and its concept is phenomenal.

The local church supplies the water for the village and so much more. There is even a simple loan plan where the church loans money to its own people for business and enterprise with the oversight of the P.E.A.C.E. church. Strong relationships are the strength behind all of this.

Out on the mission field in foreign countries the concern is that Missions trips can be feel-good trips. We show up and love on all the kids, deliver toys, give out candy, build a house or church and often (of course not always) but most often, we take our pictures and feel-good moments and leave until the next trip we may go on.

Some trips are designed for this, like building a home, or a church, or joining in with an existing group. But people out on the field say far too often we show up bringing hope, toys, candy and love, then we fill our cameras with videos and photos, and leave them, never to see them again. It's very difficult on them personally, and to the people they serve.

My father-in-law, Brother Bloomfield is in his nineties and is still building churches in India right from his home. Age has slowed him down a little but he is still helping people across the earth. How can he do this? Because of the relationships he has established over decades with the beautiful Indian people.

He built Faith And Vision Orphanages from the ground up, started medical clinics, raised orphans who have become pastors, doctors, nurses, and community leaders, training the Indian people to reach their own communities. He traveled worldwide preaching and connecting local churches to his vision and sending resources (and often taking the resources personally, more times than I could count to India) to build the many works there. He's so loved that each year on his birthday they throw a massive feast and party in his name.

I mentioned one of my mentors, Orvella Phillips who still goes on Mexico and Indian Reservation trips. She knows her people's names and knows what's going on in their lives. She makes over the Pastor's families and shows up with all their favorites.

We took some of our builders to help her finish a church on one of her Arizona reservations and the people all LOVE her. She brings them tremendous strength. She trains them to minister effectively to their own people. She brings hope to them as leaders and she always has a group of young people with her training them up! It's long lasting and true transformation out on the field.

This is the concept to keep in mind—Whenever you go out on the field, keep your eyes open and looking at what you can do for the people from the FRONTLINE when you return home to your local church.

What relationships can you build over time? What can you arrange, collaborate, or gather your church to support, long after you leave the people on the field? Could you send the Pastor/Leader's kids through school? Educate them right through college? Build a home? Send supplies? God will reveal His heart to you. Trust God to show you CONNECTIONS that will last into their future—You are with them for a beautiful purpose.

While in Cambodia, you can only imagine the vast need there is. The SHE RESCUE home does everything with absolute excellence. I felt hopeless at one point, thinking I can only do so little compared to what's needed and then Hillary said, "You know what helps us the most, consistent monthly giving. Big amounts are awesome, but it's what we can depend on that really keeps us going."

I thought, 'Well, we can do that.' We send monthly support they can depend on.

You are capable and positioned to do SO much for the Master's use. I know God is speaking to you about what you can attach yourself to, or create, to serve local and foreign mission's that He has placed within your heart...

Don't be like me and think the need is just way to massive... The sign that hangs big and bold in the SHE Rescue Home offices in Cambodia is:

"TO SUCCUMB TO THE ENORMITY OF THE PROBLEM IS TO FAIL THE ONE"

I host an AMAZING yearly Women's Conference. Many friends from big cities come and can't believe what we do in a city like ours.

I decided it's just far too blessed, beautiful, and lovely to keep to ourselves and it hit me—How can I live next door to Mexico, where women live without running water, bathrooms or electricity, and not do something about it? In fact, I can put you in my car and drive you to the Mexican border in less than 20 minutes, and another 10 minutes into Mexico, I can introduce you to "Cardboard Town." It's heartbreaking. I'll frequently be standing in Dillard's, Marshall's or Target, and think, "God bless my precious sisters who are only a half hour away in their little plumbing and electrically deficient homes, that are boiling in the desert summer and FREEZING COLD in the desert winter."

I contacted a dear Pastor friend who we support in Mexico and she agreed to let us take our "Speak Love" women's conference to Mexico.

I sent a small team of women over to assess what we needed to do to make everything special and they met with the Mexico team to plan out how it would all work out. They returned with a list and we put everything together.

We held "SPEAK LOVE" in Arizona and then arrived the next day in Mexico.

We decorated and fixed up their humble bathrooms stunningly. Next, we set up a big beautiful pamper/manicure area.

Oh—I wish you could have seen these sweet women, as they sat with their eyes closed and their arms outstretched, while one girl had each arm, applying gorgeous scented lotion, that they massaged into their freshly painted nails and hands, and another girl massaging her neck. Many were field workers, and others came from sad places, but on this night they were in Heaven! We decorated the place, and it was exhilarating as the women walked in. We had the BEST time ever.

The women responded at the altar for what felt like hours. It was so touching... They cried as we prayed for them, and they didn't want to leave God's presence. I knew not to let the night end with a heavy atmosphere, so we pulled out our huge bubble machine, flipped it on and bubbles poured into the church as we sang upbeat worship songs. We knew exactly what they were singing, we just didn't know how to pronounce the words! :)

The women went crazy; they were clapping, jumping, dancing, and singing their hearts out.

We ended the night with a full catered dinner and my favorite, massive "Tres Leches" cakes!

My Precious Pastor friend, JoDean who led the church in Mexico, passed away (breaking my heart in two!) God has now connected us to a new Pastor and his wife (I'm looking forward to building a friendship with her.) They are in an area with even greater needs—JoDean will be smiling on us!

In our next chapter, Lead For Mission, I talk about leadership and how to really pull something like this off. It's all about the team. Seriously, it's so much easier than you might think! Please hear me when I tell you it takes JUST AS MUCH EFFORT TO PLAN SOMETHING SMALL AS IT DOES TO PLAN SOMETHING BIG! So plan for BIG things! DREAM BIG! HOPE BIG... The World is waiting for you, don't keep us waiting.

BIG DREAMERS

Here are a few of my friends who dream BIG, WORK hard and enjoy the HUSTLE to make UNIQUE relationship ministry happen.

My dear mentor-friend, Dr. Maureen Anderson (thewordforwinners.com) is BEAUTIFUL and in her mid-seventies. She retired from Pastoring and has passed the torch of pastoral leadership to her two daughters-in-law, Kelli & Holly Anderson who lead their great church, Living Word Bible Church in Mesa, AZ, alongside their husbands, Senior Pastors Jason and Scot Anderson.

Dr. Maureen just begun! She has created and launched a fantastic television ministry from the ground up. She and her husband Dr. Tom (just celebrated 50 years of marriage) are creating TV stations and another new show (plus she just wrote yet another brilliant book.) Dr. Maureen's mission is the airwaves, and she is consistently connecting her network to missions and local church awareness.

My sister-heart friend Pastor Sheila Gerald never stops! She has fought human trafficking with every available resource for years. She had a mobile trailer that scanned the downtown streets of Seattle helping prostitutes.

She has a girl's home in South Africa for rescued victims and massive women's events with the soul-purpose of raising awareness and funds that are distributed in many directions. She leads teams on the other side of the rescue, responding with immediate help for victims.

I deeply admire her non-stop consistent vision to ERADICATE human trafficking! Sheila is one very STRONG powerful leader connecting her church to the RESCUE.

My stunning friend, Pastor Dianne Wilson (Newport church, CA) went through some very significant struggles in her identity as a young woman so she wrote a book, "Mirror-Mirror" and it's sweeping through the California school district and educational system empowering girls of all ages to believe in themselves.

The program is now in women's prisons and the influence of the book is growing. Dianne's mission is to empower her young team of women to lift the female heart in The Mirror-Mirror Project.

The Beautiful 1980 MISS AMERICA, Cheryl Pruitt-Salem is STUNNING in every way and a dear friend who is such a generous giver of herself along with her husband Harry. They lost their precious daughter Gabriella to heaven at just 6 years old— DEVASTATING! But they have spent their lives restoring people back to life with their own lives.

They write phenomenal books on healing from loss as they have LIVED IT! Cheryl's Mission— Taking hope and healing across the earth! ("From Mourning to Morning" is the best-book-ever.)

She is consistently strengthening the local church and connecting them to immediate causes.

My lovely 'HAPPY' friend, Audrey Meisner suffered consequences from a devastating mistake she made in her marriage. It almost took her down but instead, she decided to fight and win.

It was a long hard road causing serious unhappiness and self-hatred. But now years later she is one of the HAPPIEST girls I know! She and her wonderful husband, who gave her grace each step of the way, have a ministry to marriages and it is AMAZING! Her mission field is restoring marriages.

Pastor Jillian Chambers created an amazing worship CD of her team with proceeds going to SHE RESCUE. Pastor Penny Maxwell LOVES to cook so she has created several Southern Kitchen cook books, just for the soul purpose of helping missions. Penny is so passionate about it she is now a regular on her local morning news show as she cooks and shares her recipes and spreads her message of standing on the FRONTLINE for missions.

FRONTLINE WORLD CHANGERS: WHO'S WORLD DOES GOD WANT TO CHANGE... THROUGH YOU?

The following are real examples of Frontline women who are changing the world of some very grateful people in need of God's love and purpose in their lives:

Exercise girls use their abilities to make girls healthy; body, soul, and spirit, as outreach within their church. They then go to inner cities together for 'Fun In The Park' and hold mini-exercise camps with all the kids.

Mom's making sandwiches and going to parks in low-income areas... They feed all the little hungry kids while their own kids eat and all play together. They pause and share stories of Jesus and hope with pictures and little songs.

Women collecting Prom dresses and throwing big 'Get Glamourous' parties in their churches. They give dresses to teens, military wives, and brides (We don't require our girls to return the dress, shoes, or jewelry; nor do they pay a fee—It's all on the house with our Cinderella Project.)

Gather all your glamour-makers together and throw one fun party!!

'Glamour Girls' for sweet older lonely ladies in homes. Gather some girls together and go have a pamper day at your local 'old-folks home'. It may not sound too glamorous, but it is in the Master's eyes. Just take a walk down the halls like I did a while back... The sad loneliness will envelop you and your heart will BREAK, and you'll remember why you do this—glamour or not... You will put a smile on God's face and such HAPPINESS in your women's hearts.

Actors and directors, creating stage and cinema to inspire the world with God's love. I oversee a yearly massive outdoor Christmas Production (we live in the desert).

'Jesus Is Born' is a HUGE undertaking with wardrobe, makeup, hair/wig, set-building, media, lighting, backstage, live animal handlers, marketing, soundtrack developers...

It's a substantial connection of creative people to our community. We also do a yearly 'Galactic Show' (which used to be a Pirate Show) with a large cast and crew. We have developed many other incredible leaders for this.

It's performed at our city wide A M A Z I N G PUMPKIN PATCH that hosts tens of thousands of people each year. I know... We are crazy BIG thinkers and DO-ER'S of what I'm writing to you.

Just ask yourself, "How can I take what I do and connect it to God's House? How can I build a relationship to others outside in our community?" God will show you as He showed me. I look around and see, my years in the film industry while living in Vancouver, Canada, is all around me, being used for God and His House.

Entrepreneurs and enterprises selling products that financially support LOCAL CHURCH and MISSIONS.

Kingdom Builders are SO NEEDED. I know MANY churches where entrepreneurs get together and create businesses and train young business minded people for financially strengthening the local church and Missions.

They start businesses like Coffee Shops, Park and Ride lots, Thrift stores, Marketing businesses, and so many more and... Yes—even Pumpkin Patches :)

Hairdressers gathering together, doing back to school cut-a-thons and giving each child a backpack full of school supplies....

I have to make myself stop right here... as I could go on and on... SO MANY WIDE-OPEN DOORS... Just pick one and do it! I once heard such a true statement that revolutionized my thinking:

'IF YOU ARE TRYING TO FIGURE OUT GOD'S WILL FOR YOUR LIFE, FIND A NEED AND FILL IT, AND YOU'LL BE STANDING RIGHT IN THE MIDDLE OF GOD'S WILL.'

I continually watch God bring out FRONTLINE WOMEN'S beautiful best as they serve Him with their whole hearts.

SERVE ON LOVELY LADY!

For this reason I remind you to fan into flame the gift of God... For the Spirit God gave us does not make us timid, but gives us power, love and self-discipline.

2 Timothy 1:7 (NIV)

FRONTLINE DISCUSSION

How has this chapter spoken to you and inspired you to FRONTLINE action?

How were you challenged to think of your Mission in a fresh way?

What do you feel God is Calling YOU to do? What if you had ZERO limitations?

FRONTLINE PRAYER

Dear Jesus, HERE I AM, SEND ME!   I'm anticipating the doors You are opening for me and I ask for Your favor!   Your Word says in John 12:26 that as I serve You, our Heavenly Father will honor and reward me. I thank You for that honor and reward. I know You are arranging connections in heavenly places that will happen here on earth. I'm READY and I'm WILLING to be used by You!

Now spend just a few moments quietly... listening... What is Jesus speaking to you?

Pray for your church and the mission relationships they currently have. Ask God to increase these connections and ask Him to awaken in your heart where you can be involved, or be the connector and possibly lead.

FRONTLINE CONFESSION

I'm a HISTORY MAKER! I take on BIG ADVENTURES using who I am, what I do and my life experiences to EXPAND GOD'S KINGDOM HERE ON EARTH. I'm being used by my Master Jesus Christ and I LOVE IT. My eyes and my heart are open to how God is moving and I'm right in the middle of it. I live an extraordinary fabulous faith life! Faith without works is dead BUT FAITH WITH WORKS IS ALIVE AND MIRACULOUS. I expect miracles, believe for miracles and walk in the divine blessing of God, look—it's all around me.

SCRIPTURES TO BUILD YOUR FAITH

John 12:26; Jude 3-4

Matthew 5:13-16; Revelations 14:6

Acts 1:5-8; 2 Corinthians 2:15-16

Frontline Woman

Chapter Eight

LEAD FOR MISSION

Every FRONTLINE WOMAN is called to lead on the line where God has strategically placed her. You may not see yourself as a leader but it's high time you embraced your own personal leadership, and step up to lead your mission well, with passion.

Leadership is simply using what you've invested in yourself and helping others with it.

I heard a dear friend of mine, Pastor Holly Wagner (God Chicks) say years ago, "Every woman should have one hand in the hand of a mentor and her other hand in the hand of one she is mentoring."

I have held onto this and have determined to make sure my life is consistently supported and shaped by mentors, women I want to be like and live out the results they create.

I then surround myself with women who want to be led and mentored in their FRONTLINE life. Leadership and mentorship are closely related. I look at it like this,

- Leadership is vision, direction and accomplishing greatness together
- Mentorship is training, developing and preparation you give/get to accomplish greatness together.

It's important to develop a well-rounded approach to both leadership and mentorship in your FRONTLINE life. Sometimes you'll lead a big group and other times it will be one on one. Remember, leading for mission is about serving— Serving your Master, your mission, and those you are leading.

Here are 10 of my favorite leadership and mentorship keys for you to master as you become the FRONTLINE leader God has entrusted you to be.

1. SHARPEN YOUR SKILLS

If the ax is dull, and one does not sharpen the edge,
Then he must use more strength; but wisdom brings success.

Ecclesiastes 10:10 (NKJ)

We expand and develop our abilities to have more to GIVE of ourselves—more to SHARE with the world, and we have more of ourselves to LOVE with.

Power on the FRONTLINE is purposefully choosing to learn, sharpen, and strengthen our leadership/mentorship abilities. It's time to get 'BIG' SPIRITED... God is ready to do more with you.

Don't let the season you are in hinder you from developing more of who you are to give away more of who you become. And don't let your mission find you unprepared to step out in faith with the knowledge and practical experience you will need.

A secret to sharpening your skills is following the David promotion pattern: He could only step up to the challenge of the giant with faith and confidence because he knew he had already fought and won lesser battles with a bear and a lion.

You can practice for the throne long before you make it out of the field.

Prove and expand your leadership skill by leading now where you are. Take on the challenge of being a volunteer leader and develop the skills you will undoubtedly require for your mission.

2. SHARE WITH GOD IN PRAYER

The prayer of a (FRONTLINE) woman
— gets the job done!

James 5:16 (Paraphrased)

Give time to talk to God every day. Even if it's just moments at first... Soon it will grow longer each day as the demand of leadership on your life will require it.

You are so valuable to your Master and He wants to be with you to strengthen you and teach you His ways as you talk to him... about EVERYTHING. Just invite Him right into every area of your life, this will empower you greatly. You will become SO strong in the presence of Jesus... So BIG spirited—just be with Him every day.

3. GOD WILL SHARE WITH YOU IN HIS WORD

God's Word is alive and powerful. It is sharper than the sharpest two-edged sword, cutting between soul and spirit, between joint and marrow. It exposes our innermost thoughts and intensions of the heart.

Hebrews 4:12 (NLT)

You might be a Bible app user but I want to encourage you to have a physical Bible you can hold, read, and love its well-worn pages. God will speak tender things to you in His word. As it teaches you and touches you, mark it and let teardrops fall and bleed the ink you wrote upon it.

Learn where passages are that you love, write what God speaks, date it for reminiscing and memorize it to empower! Consider a Bible reading plan and read the entire Bible.

4. NEXT LEVEL WORSHIP

Shout for joy to the Lord, worship the Lord with gladness; come before him with joyfulness.

Psalm 100:2 (NIV)

It's challenge time dear FRONTLINE friend. It's time to worship your Savior with fresh passion.

Worship is a lifestyle and sharpening your worship skills will intensify your FRONTLINE life. Let these habits become a part of who you are as a FRONTLINE WOMAN:

- Arrive at God's House on time (early!) Sunday starts on Saturday night. Protect your Sunday morning by doing a few things prior, the night before, to eliminate the strife that can take place to get out the door.
- Serve regularly—It's time to get involved. No more sidelines. You are FRONTLINE ready.
- When the music begins for worship, be the first to stand and sing from your heart. You will be leading worship right from your seat.
- Give with expectation and happiness.
- Open God's Word and read along as your Pastor preaches.
- Take notes. Be alert to what God is asking you to participation.

These few steps will take your worship life to a whole new level.

5. GET MENTORED BY THE BEST

*The things you have learned and received
and heard and seen in me, practice these things,
and the God of peace will be with you.*

Philippians4:9

FRONTLINE WOMEN who lead and mentor are continually developing and evolving into greatness.

I always remind women, earbuds can be your university for ANYTHING. You can learn to build any skill or develop any personal achievement by plugging in and downloading knowledge. There is nonstop information to grow your spirit and enlarge your capacity that you can listen to anywhere at any time. Someone can mentor you that you never even meet in your lifetime just by listening and learning from their products.

If you are in school, take purposeful classes that develop who you are. Most high schools offer students a program, including college credits or even a dual graduate degree. This takes hustle and hard work but it's so worth it.

PLEASE do NOT go into debt for an education if you can avoid it. It may seem like FREE money but it is NOT, and every penny will roll around behind you forever until it's paid back. If you need a degree to do what you desire to do, please make sure the pay rate will be great enough to pay your student loan(s) off and live the lifestyle you desire.

6. COMPELLING COMMUNICATION

Let your conversation be always full of grace, seasoned with salt, so that you may know how to answer everyone.

Colossians 4:6 (NIV)

It's not 'what you say' but HOW you say it, that will lead people in your Mission or mentor those who are following you. Highly influential leaders are never bossy, pushy or rude, EVER!!!!! A good leader never needs to express any of those traits. Compelling communication begins way before an order is ever given.

I have seen SO many leaders RUIN their influence and destroy their leadership with a bossy, rude, attitude, assuming their position gives them the right to demand people do what they want. I've sadly watched this way too many times. You can't get people to DO anything with this approach, whether it's volunteers or paid staff.

Often females who lead men will adopt a masculine mindset rather than staying in her God-given femininity. Unfortunately, culture has taught women that equality means proving she can do what a man does and even better. She has NO IDEA how she is robbing herself from God's best for her mission. This is not a competition but an opportunity to respect a man's masculinity and lead him to use it to its greatest potential.

This understanding will help you have fantastic relationships with the men you lead. It is NOT weakness, belittling, or betraying your own strength, but actually, it's a sign of strength when you can allow men to be who God created them to be.

LOVE YOUR PEOPLE BEFORE YOU LEAD YOUR PEOPLE

I mean really love them by accepting who they are at face value. Where do they come from? What are their strengths, weaknesses, hopes and maybe their fears? Whenever you walk past them, acknowledge them with a sincere touch. Learn their names with word pictures. (There's a couple whose names just would not sink into my heart so I envisioned David Cassidy and Shirley Jones from the Partridge family ((I'm so dating myself)) but I never forgot their names again and I love them today more than ever!)

It's true that "people buy into YOU before they buy into your vision."

Always remember, people want to follow you to do something amazing, so lead them to it by being positive, uplifting them, and showing love.

Jesus said, "love the Lord your God with all your heart and all your soul and with all your mind. This is the first and greatest commandment. The second is like it; Love everyone as you love yourself.

Matthew 22:37-39 (NIV)

7. DEVELOP PEOPLE

Join together in following my example, brothers and sisters, and just as you have us as a model, keep your eyes on those who live as we do.

Philippians 3:17 (NIV)

People will lay their lives down with you when you help them develop into the best versions of themselves. They will rise up to what you believe they are capable of achieving. I live this out almost daily and it is astonishing to experience. There are people around me who started out small on the inside with no confidence or voice to do what they are doing now. Many are living out their FRONTLINE potential in huge ways because a leader mentored and invested in them.

Learn how to have conversations that let people know what you see within them, then teach, train, and stand back, and watch them do amazing things.

Always remember, when you oversee someone doing what you trained them for the first time, find something to gently correct them on. This will keep them open to you developing them and knowing you will bring out their best.

When needed, have hard conversations about bad attitudes, negative actions or any area you know needs a change.

My mom could tell you off and challenge you to your core and you'd walk out feeling fantastic about yourself. Her technique—She would first talk about how amazing you are then she'd slide right into how the behavior you have is hindering you from your greatness, and end with where she saw your amazing self going.

She'd pray an incredible prayer for you and her words would paint this amazing picture of who you were becoming in God and then send you on your way. You'd leave happy and ready to take on life!

Her brilliant formula has become part of who I am as a leader and I seem to (almost) always get a big thank you following my hard conversations.

People need to know how much you care, and they will go to the ends of the earth with you.

> *And Jesus kept increasing in wisdom and stature,*
> *and in favor with God and men.*
> *Luke 2:52 (NIV)*

8. CONSISTENCY

Appreciate your pastoral leaders who gave you the Word of God. Take a good look at the way they live, and let their faithfulness instruct you, as well as their truthfulness. There should be a consistency that runs through us all.

For Jesus doesn't change—yesterday, today, tomorrow,
he's always totally himself.

Hebrews 13:7 (MSG)

This is one of the most powerful tools for leadership. Your family, friends, co-workers, teams, and all who you associate with must see you being consistent. You can't be up one day and then down the next—regularly. You can't be mad at everyone for every little thing and then punish them with your behavior.

We all have our ups and downs but as FRONTLINE leaders we can't let our moods, tiredness, or heaviness show too often. There is a place for it, but not when you are leading. People we are leading really don't want to know our challenges. They have enough of their own.

Get a small, purposefully chosen, support team around you where you can cry it out, then LET IT GO. When you are leading your tribe, be your consistent, dependable self. You will see a huge change in the people you are leading when they trust who you consistently are. Keep your vision stable and don't change it like the wind.

Settle in your heart what you are doing and do it as unto the Lord.

> *Work with enthusiasm, as though you*
> *were working for the Lord rather than people.*
> *Ephesians 6:7 (NLT)*

9. POSITIVITY

> *Summing it all up, friends, I'd say you'll do best by filling*
> *your minds and meditating on things true, noble, reputable,*
> *authentic, compelling, gracious—the best, not the worst; the*
> *beautiful, not the ugly; things to praise, not things to curse.*
> *Put into practice what you learned from me, what you heard*
> *and saw and realized. Do that, and God, who makes*
> *everything work together, will work you into his most*
> *excellent harmonies.*

> *Philippians 4:8 (MSG)*

Our first FRONTLINE woman Eve was deceived by one word, DISSATISFACTION. Eve was God's first perfectly created woman living in perfect conditions. The serpent goes to her and the first thing he does is cast doubt in her heart towards God and about her life. He says, "Eat the forbidden fruit because there is MORE than what you already have and you can have more, and be more, just like God. Eat for MORE, Eve. Become all knowing. Get it ALL."

Her dissatisfaction with what she had, gave her the 'I WANT MORE' appetite, and it TOOK HER DOWN. The serpent got her to think negatively about her heavenly Father and it devastated her entire life, and ours too.

You must train yourself to FIGHT NEGATIVITY EVERY STEP OF THE WAY. It's the most evil thing that will bring a FRONTLINE leader down.

So many amazing, good-hearted, lovely leaders are wiped out by becoming negative. It often begins with turning negative towards our leaders. We feel our Pastors or leaders don't support us. We complain, speak our discontentment to others and get dissatisfied, wanting MORE. Our appetite grows, and we get deceived into thinking our leaders aren't giving us enough of "MORE" of what WE WANT.

We can end up hurting SO many precious people on the FRONTLINE around us, all because we got dissatisfied. I've watched this up close. Pastors are people called by God to lead, and none of us will do it perfectly. You absolutely must give your leaders a break and stay positive towards them.

Shut off the voice of 'YOU DESERVE MORE.' If something is not right, resolve it right away, so it does not grow into dissatisfaction and take you down. It can end up devastating your FRONTLINE life.

Stay positive about the people you serve as a leader. Stop getting so mad when someone is late, or they didn't do this or that.

Think about it... that's why YOU are the leader and they are not. They have a long way to go yet. Too many leaders waste their precious time to serve, love, and lead, being mad at their team or even other leaders.

You should confront negative behavior, but if you're mad about something it means you haven't dealt with it. In fact, you're probably mad at yourself for not correcting the issue. Lead with vision, demand responsibility from your team members based on "why we do this", but stay positive and proactive. Stay the leader.

How do you stay positive and passionate about your FRONTLINE life when it is tough, discouraging, and painful?

Hear me well... BECOME GRATEFUL within the situation... It really is as easy as that. Nothing will change your perspective more than looking through the lens of gratitude. It takes a little practice, and now you know it, you can master it!

Never stop praying. Be thankful in all circumstances, for this is God's will for you who belong to Jesus.

1 Thessalonians 5:18 (NLT)

10. START WHERE YOU ARE

[Those] whose delight is in the law of the Lord, and who meditates on his law day and night. That person is like a tree planted by streams of water, which yields its fruit in season and whose leaf does not wither—whatever they do prospers.

Psalms 1:2-3 (NIV)

If you are a new bride, take time to learn your man and become an amazing wife so one day you will lead other new wives. If you have been married for more than1 month, you can already help lead engaged future brides.

If you are a mommy, we celebrate you! What a gift and a challenge, all mixed into one of the greatest character builders of all! Learn motherhood and be a wonderful mommy so when that season is through, you can help new mamas.

If you have a one-month-old baby you are already a leader/mentor. Help pregnant moms, even if it's just one mama, let her into your life (dirty diapers, messy home and all) and lead her into her new season.

If you have a child with learning challenges, disabilities, illnesses, autism, or mental health issues... Please be strong and know we love you and need you to learn all you can so one day you may turn to bless, teach and empower other parents to overcome. Journal daily, even if for a few minutes, to remember what you are learning and walking out. You very well may write a book one day. We need it desperately! In the meantime keep strong, we are with you.

If you are a career girl, shoot for the top in resources so you can have an abundance to finance ministry goals. If you've rocked a position for one month or more, you can help unemployed women find their dream job. (Consider sales so your income is not capped but you have unlimited financial potential). Teach women how to pursue, present, and persuade employers for positions. They need you!

If you are the mom of teens, you must learn this season well because these can be hard (but wonderful) times! Our hearts are with you!! Best book EVER, "How To Really Love Your Teenager" By Ross Campbell. No book like it. He has several, and he is always updating it to keep up with our changing times, so get the most recent edition. You will thrive with his knowledge. Then LOVE and help other mamas of teens. We need you.

If you are in the season of elderly parent care, we are with you all the way. What precious (but often most difficult) season with so much to learn. The Lord promises us the reward for honoring our parents is a long life that goes well. (Ephesians 6:2-3) When this season has ended you will be a huge strength to others enduring their very hard season and they will greatly value what you've achieved.

If you find yourself in the unbelievable heartbreak of the loss of a spouse or even worse a child, hold on we NEED you. You WILL get through this and we will cherish your tender care and invaluable advice and help during our seasons of loss. No one or nothing will last forever here on earth so when it's gone we'll grasp onto you and what you've endured.

Learn the lessons of whatever season you are in, but don't stand still or wait for the next season... You'll always be waiting. Develop your abilities and become all you can NOW, in this season.

FRONTLINE DISCUSSION

What is your strongest of the 5 Leadership keys? What makes you think you are strong in this area and why?

What is the one you need to work on the most and why?

Recount a time you chose to say positive in a negative leadership situation.

What was the outcome?

FRONTLINE PRAYER

Dear Father God, I ask that You help me to step up and be the leader You've created me to be. I ask that You direct me in how to best sharpen my skills so I'm fully equipped for my mission.

Help me to communicate with grace and love to all who You choose for me to lead.

I ask that You bless the people I lead and help me to see the BEST that you placed within each of them. Help me to learn balance so I stay consistent with my attitudes and moods.

Guide me to close friends I can trust to share my heart with, helping me stay strong. I thank You for trusting me with a leading life, and I will lead well. I want to pause and really thank You for ...

FRONTLINE CONFESSION

'I am a FRONTLINE LEADING WOMAN who is always growing and sharpening my skills.

I choose to learn during every season of my life. I am a compelling communicator drawing the best out of the people I lead. My team know I love them. I have a consistent character and I inspire, uplift, and point out the best in everyone and everything! I live a leading life of gratitude and happiness!

SCRIPTURES TO BUILD YOUR FAITH FOR LEADERSHIP

Galatians 6:9; Isiah 41:10; Proverbs 11:14

Philippians 2:3-4; 2 Timothy 2:15; Luke 6:31

Mark 10:42-45; Proverbs 4:23; Hebrews 13:17

Chapter Nine

STRENGTH FOR MISSION

Stay alert! Watch out for your great enemy, the devil.
He prowls around like a roaring lion,
looking for someone to devour
1 Peter 5:8 (NLT)

You now know what a DANGEROUS FORCE for the Master's use you are. You are invaluable, and you must guard and protect your valuable self by being fully aware the enemy is ALWAYS lurking around to bring you down. He is relentless and will use every opportunity to destroy you and make your heart give up. He'll hunt you like a lion and when he sees you in a season of struggle, he will roar so utterly loud it will distract you from noticing God's miraculous hand that's protecting you and guiding you. The enemy's ultimate goal is to weaken the line by knocking you over and out.

YOU, precious warrior woman, are in the vast "company" of FRONTLINE WOMEN, and there is A LOT OF US... You must always remember you are NEVER ALONE. We are in this together with our Master Jesus Christ who NEVER LEAVES US OR ABANDONS US—EVER. Before we even enter into a heartache season, He's already there! The very last words Jesus spoke to us when He left for heaven are...

"I am with you ALWAYS... even to the very end of the world!"

How utterly powerful is this forever reminder—JESUS IS WITH YOU ALWAYS!!

On my give up day I was completely DONE! I had totally QUIT! I was FINISHED! The enemy was roaring so loudly all I could think was death thoughts. His claws were deep in my flesh and I had absolutely NO FIGHT LEFT IN ME. I laid in my bed in St. Paul's Hospital in Vancouver, British Columbia, completely hopeless. I was over and I was out!

THIS FRONTLINE WOMAN WAS SHATTERED

I was pretty much bald, weighed well under 80lbs and I hurt all over, inside and out. My tears were completely dried up... I don't think my body could create one more... My cheeks were rose hot red, and all I wanted to do was breathe my last breath and surrender.

I closed my eyes tightly as the sun pierced through my window. "God, I CANNOT do this... Please... I quit... I'm finished."

Nine months prior I had barely survived an acute attack of ulcerative colitis (I was at the life-threatening stage of a totally infected bowel). You would NOT believe the utter hell I faced and what it took to fight for my life, in and out of the hospital for months... And the devastation my precious husband and two little sons endured was unthinkable...

We just could not gain control of the infection and I was sinking quickly, going to the bathroom well over 20 times a day with pain that felt like labor and gushes of blood that just would not stop. I was a living skeleton with shriveled grey skin and I realized I had come to the end of myself.

Even though I was a pitiful sight, I did all I could to KEEP MY FIGHT UP AND DRAW ON GOD'S POWER to make it through. I'm not saying for one minute it was easy but this FRONTLINE WOMAN fought as hard as she could!

My Bible NEVER LEFT MY HOSPITAL BED, either it was on my chest while I slept, under my pillow, or by my side. I wrote EVERY healing scripture and story I could find inside it and quoted healing passages out of a little book that a dear friend drove three hours to bring me called "By His Stripes". I was one well-armored warrior, and it SAVED MY LIFE. The doctor told me, "I've never had a patient quite like you. I had a bloke once who was on the fence and survived but you definitely have surprised me. It's extraordinary, actually."

I finally had won to the point of being able to be at home and slowly I was myself again. My husband quit having to carry me up the stairs due to such weakness and then the day came when I achieved my summer long goal.

I walked my little son Stetson to his first day of first grade, with my baby Sterling in the stroller. I was thrilled!

Oh, and a side note, during all of this my mom was dying of ovarian cancer... HELLISH STUFF.

After nine months of being well, early one morning I felt the colitis stirring inside my body and my heart sunk... I heard as clear as a bell, "It's time for surgery. It's not a failure, and it has nothing to do with your faith. I will be with you every step of the way." Ughhh... I was soooo despondent... It wasn't what I wanted to hear, but I was done with this disease.

Faith to totally trust God dropped into my heart. I knew God was up to something. Just two days later my dear friend, Doctor Karen Hendrickson, who had delivered my first son and then moved onto the mission field, was home on furlough from Africa.

She looked at me across the table at lunch and said, "What's been going on with you, you just aren't yourself." After pouring my heart out, within 24 hours she had me downtown Vancouver in a top surgeon's office who had created a surgical technique called the J-Pouch. It's where the bowel is completely removed and the intestines are pulled from your body, cut into sixes, and a reservoir is created into a J-shape... Just like the plumbing under the kitchen sink. It's the same concept. The doctor decided, as a favor to his friend Dr. Hendrickson, he would fit me in. Because he was retiring, I was literally his very last patient. (Thank you, Jesus, for Doctor Atkinson and my sweet Doctor Hendrickson!) Since I had been so sick the doctor decided to do my surgery in two steps. First, to remove my bowel, and then nine months later, do the second surgery to create the J-pouch.

So there I now laid after surgery one, in the hospital, with my entire bowel removed. Oh... I had big faith, and I was all on board to have this horribly diseased organ cut out, but now there was no turning back. That's when the enemy roared with all his might, drowning out my spirit of faith, and I was sure he had won.

There was a painful stitch line that stretched from my pelvis bone, just around my belly button and all the way up under my sternum. I reached my hands under the covers and my hand gently ran down the right side of my tummy bumping into my newly created stoma, wrapped in a big plastic medical bag. It was hot, hurting and SO devastatingly disfiguring.... "NO!!!   I'M NOT DOING THIS ONE!   IT'S TOO MUCH AND I CAN'T! I HATE MYSELF!!!"

And I truly did at that moment...

I hated me. All I could think of was how my poor husband was married to a deformed, bald, total loser!   The newly released song by Rod Stewart, "Have I Told You Lately That I Love You," rang in my head as Stephen would sing it to me... I screamed inside myself, NO STEPHEN!! DON'T LOVE ME. HOW CAN YOU LOVE ME??!!!

It was the day the Ostomy nurse was coming to train me how to deal with my stoma and I was having no part of it... not this girl. I just couldn't. It devastated me. A stoma is the end of your intestine that's brought through the lower area of your abdomen. It's turned inside out and then sewn onto your tummy's skin.

This is a WONDERFUL life-saving surgery, bypassing the need for a bowel, allowing digested food to spill out into an ostomy bag.

At first, because of the trauma, the stoma is very inflamed, swollen, and painful. It moves around a lot and the sensation is really evident and really weird... At this moment I could have cared less that it was a 'wonderful' life-saving surgery. I decided I hated everything about it... and I hated me.

Laying in my hospital bed, I slowly opened my eyes. Somehow I had mustered up tears again, and they slid down the sides of my temples onto my head, because I had no hair to soak them up. I leaned over to reach for a tissue when I saw that the sun was peering right in on my new fluffy pink slippers that my dear Stephen had made sure I had.

They were so pretty and soft looking they actually ministered to me. I closed my eyes and cried all the more pulling myself painfully around in the sit up position they had taught me the day before. I took a deep breath, and I gently slid one foot into my pretty slipper and whispered... "Thank You"... then the next foot... "Jesus!" Out of nowhere this immense power flooded over me. I cannot explain it (Ughhhh... I still cry when I tell this story.)

The Lord spoke very clearly at that moment. He told me not to think about the vast large picture of everything but to only live in the now, and to stay GRATEFUL for the present moment I was in... "Don't think about later, just be in the right here and the right now. I'm ALWAYS right here with you in your present moment."

PLEASE ALWAYS REMEMBER FRONTLINE WOMAN, Your Master Jesus Christ is with you in your EVERY PRESENT MOMENT! You need not ask Him to do anything... HE IS DOING IT... THANK HIM IN THE NOW MOMENT!

Thankfulness and gratitude will always bring you unexplainable happiness! The Joy of the Lord is your strength... Why do you think the enemy does all he can to deceive you in your seasons of sadness... Because when you are sad, you are weak, and when you are weak, you are vulnerable to QUITTING, and If you quit, the entire FRONTLINE is weakened... Not just you, but all of us... You are vitally needed! Don't quit! Don't give up. KEEP THANKFUL Beautiful FRONTLINE girl. (Nehemiah 8:10)

Slowly I accepted God's words to me... The power of God filled my room and my gratitude became heartfelt. My heart became brave and slowly I took a stand in my pink slippers. They felt so lovely, softly padding my skinny little bony feeties. As I stood as straight as I could, I decided I could NOT give up... I just couldn't. This amazing sense of my MASTER'S call on my life was as true as I had ever known before.

God kept saying, "Stay grateful Cindy, stay grateful. I'm right here in your now-moment, and I love you!"

The MORE GRATEFUL I WAS, THE HAPPIER I BECAME AND THE HAPPIER I BECAME, THE STRONGER I FELT, AND IT COMPLETELY DROWNED OUT THE ROAR OF THE EVIL ONE!

GRATEFULNESS, PRECIOUS FRONTLINE SISTER, is your Master's key to unlock His Father's strength for you! Don't you EVER let divorce, death, prison, abortions, failure, sickness, heartache, pain, homosexuality, deformity, falling away, gender questioning, addiction, being bullied, rape, incest, cyber mishaps, molestation, domestic violence, eating disorders, learning disability, labels, early sex, sex out of marriage, rejection, foster home, panic attacks, ADD, ADHD, autism, porn, jealousy, self-comparison, FEAR, and whatever else is HAUNTING you, KEEP you from a FRONTLINE LIFE, FULL OF GRATITUDE!

It does not matter WHAT YOU HAVE BEEN IN, OR ARE IN—No FRONTLINE WOMAN is perfect. We have ALL been afflicted in this world of injustice and darkness. Not one of us has it all together. We each must continue to strive to lead with a pure heart, but the devil is a devourer, and he assumes if he can find you tangled in a mess he can condemn you, and roar you RIGHT OFF THE FRONTLINE—No!!! Not you... No matter what, YOU CAN ALWAYS FIND YOUR WAY OUT WITH A GRATEFUL HEART... and a grateful heart becomes a HAPPY HEART that is STRONG and able to get through ANYTHING.

Later that morning as I was waiting for my nurse I heard him... You can always hear my father-in-law before you see him. He was loudly praying and saying, "Hello Love" to all the nurses... My heart leaped with excitement, "It's Papa Bloomfield", my evangelist father-in-law.

He had been out-of-town preaching somewhere and I never even expected him, especially early in the day.

He walked right into my doorway, turned and pointed at me, "Lovie, the Lord woke me up and told me, 'go see Cindy...' Listen to me! Your testimony will go across the earth. You can do this, and you will share this to hurting people all over the world! This is your message, this is your mission."

These were his exact words and then he stomped his foot and said, 'WHOOP GLORY' three times! I was sooooo happy, and of course, I cried again as God was showing me that a heart of gratitude releases the miraculous and ANYTHING CAN HAPPEN! While I was trusting Jesus through my pain, He woke up my Papa B and sent him to me.

Later that afternoon an angel appeared to me... her name was Nurse Mariette Carman (I LOVE NURSES). She took one look at me and knew just how to whip me into shape. She took me into the bathroom as I told her, "Ok, so I'm gonna try all this but I'm so sorry, I just don't know if I can do it." She said, "Oh shoot, I should have brought my blind patient in to meet you, he was just here and he could have told you how great he is doing."

Blind? He was blind! And I have a challenge? Right.

I had SO much to be grateful for as Mariette taught me exactly how to handle everything. She gave me the best products that even had velvet on them and beautifully scented items and sprays. She taught me self-love at my ugliest, and this FRONTLINE girl drew on her worst give-up-day, and learned that gratefulness can get you THROUGH anything... I've NEVER had a give-up-day since, even through my second major surgery to connect everything up.

Oh... I've been hurt, sad, sick, lost, betrayed, devastatingly snubbed, brokenhearted, disappointed, forgotten, and so much more, but NEVER-EVER a give up moment because no matter what...

WE ALWAYS HAVE SOMETHING TO BE GRATEFUL FOR because GOD IS ALWAYS WORKING! There is ALWAYS HAPPINESS when the weeping is done. There is always a song in the morning. (Psalm 30:5)

I must end my story here and tell you just five weeks after my surgery I had to go nurse my mom with the SAME surgery, as the ovarian cancer she was suffering with, blocked her bowel off. It's something so deeply incomprehensible to me that I don't talk about it much. Maybe one day I'll write it all out. Just before my second surgery, she went to Heaven... SHE TAUGHT ME SO MUCH about being a FRONTLINE WARRIOR WOMAN during the end of life.

She said, "I asked God, what the heck am I gonna do? The doctor just told me I'm a dead duck! The Lord simply spoke and told me to go until I can't go any more... So that's just what I'm gonna dang-well do Cindy, I'm gonna go till I reach Heaven."

She was so vibrant that even in her most somber moments she had us laughing. She kept strong, as she'd throw her wig on because chemo took her hair, and go lead the worship at their inner-city church. She'd take her young musicians to get their music lessons, she led her kid's choir, and she went until she couldn't go anymore. At her end, I arrived from Canada and she went to heaven in about an hour, as my dad and I loved her all the way there.

When my mom's headstone was placed on her grave my mom's young, church choir kids, wanted to go see her grave and bring her flowers. So my dad loaded them up and took them.

One young African American girl immediately bent down and laid her body out flat with her face in the grass and cried, "Ms. Marilyn... Ms. Marilyn...

I LOVE YOU, MS. Marilyn!   I MISS YOU." She cried and cried... Now that's a FRONTLINE honor moment rarely seen. Our honor will be there too, long after our service for our Master on earth has been completed.

A few years ago my father stopped into a place he never goes, in the area of the church that my parents pastored. Suddenly he heard, "Pastor Dave!" He turned around and the mother of the sweet girl who had cried on my Mama's grave was running over to him and said, "Oh... Pastor Dave, I have been praying to find you!   I have to tell you, you would be so proud of my girl. She is NOW THE WORSHIP LEADER at our church and my son plays the drums there too!   They are both involved in everything for the Lord."

My dad was SO blessed, this was not a coincidence; nothing is with God! My dad needed to hear this, as both he and my mom served God with their whole hearts at Celebration Church in Downey, California. This ministered deeply to all of us. NEVER UNDERESTIMATE your service on the FRONTLINE. Never! Ever!

Hold tightly in your heart the knowledge that FRONTLINE WOMEN battle through to the end and NEVER GIVE UP... My mom battled even through her darkest hour because there was a generation she was called to lead and train up... even to the end.

YOU have a generation to lead, a tribe who SO desperately needs you. It's no longer about you— it's selflessness... FRONTLINE WOMEN may be pushed around, knocked down, gossiped about, left, broken, busted, and disgusted, but she is NEVER FINISHED.

Like our Foster mom on the first page of this book... it's all SO MUCH BIGGER THAN JUST US and our challenges, and ITS SO WORTH THE BATTLE, that goes well into the future.

I can't end my story or my book without mentioning my number one Peaceful Warrior by my side, my Stephen's mother, Althea, who we all call Mum.

She knows her Master Jesus Christ and LOVES Him with her whole being. Her message is unconditional LOVE and her mission is to help anyone who needs her, she is always right there.

She is the strongest FRONTLINE WOMAN I know.

I frequently get asked where my big spirit comes from. I don't really see it up close but I'd have to say if I do, it comes from many incredible people. Other than my amazing daddy Dave McCoy, and my feisty momma Marilyn, I've gained so much of who I am from my precious Mum Bloomfield, and of course my Papa, Brother Ray Bloomfield.

My Mum nursed me, fed me, held me, cried with me, encouraged me, sang to me, and nourished me back to life more than once through my horrible endeavor. Never once have I seen her be mean, rude, or out of character. She is constantly loving, ALWAYS! She is eternally grateful for every little thing in life, and her happiness changes you in minutes. She's always been that way... I strive to be like her.

Recently we were with our family, and on our last night, Stephen took me to go say goodbye to Mum who is now in a home as her mind has slowed down. She was at the dining table looking at her food as the nurse who helps her eat had not arrived.

I sat down next to her as Stephen grabbed a chair, "Hello Love" says Mum, as her mind has not changed how utterly sweet she is.

I reached over and took her fork and scooped food onto it, "Here Mum," and I fed her. Tears flooded my eyes as I quickly pulled myself together. I got to feed My precious Mum... Just as she had fed me. I can't tell you the honor I felt at that moment... and of course she thanked me over and over as her heart of gratitude overflowed and she smiled and laughed and made everyone around her happy.

Darlene, my beautiful Sister-in-law, who is married to my Stephen's brother Philip, pastor of Calvary Grace Church, in Surrey, B.C. Canada, ministers at her church, and at her hairdressing chair, loving people all day. She nursed, loved, and took care of our Mum's every need for several years before she went into the home. Mum had a fall, otherwise, Darlene would still be taking care of her. She chose to honor Mum's FRONTLINE Heritage that has changed us all.

Frontline Woman

Darlene is a FRONTLINE WOMAN to be honored, and her service to one of our finest is written in the pages of God's History book... Some things are eternal and not meant for earthly fame.

My precious daughter-in-love Cristina, who is married to our Stetson, is the mother of Asher and our only little Bloomfield girl (yet), Ariela Reign. Cristina is a FRONTLINE WOMAN in fashion as an Instagram personality and she is quite the influencer... What a beauty-girl, I'm so proud of her.

Our Asher is on the spectrum in his early years, and Cristina is embracing her role in raising him well and helping other Mamas of kids facing the same special needs challenges.

I know her influence will soar. I want her and Ariela to always know the FRONTLINE WOMEN whose shoulders they stand on.

My other precious daughter-in-love Jade, who is married to our Sterling, is the mother of Luke and soon to be born, little brother Zeke. I'm sure more baby Bloomfields are to come. She has such a unique entrepreneur spirit at such a young age and has begun her first company, of many

I'm sure. She also runs God's House with such passion and organization. There seems to be no challenge this girl cannot take on and achieve. She's a FRONTLINE Woman for God's House and I'm so blessed by her. I want her to forever draw on the strength of the FRONTLINE Women who have gone before her.

My beautiful niece Amanda who is the most phenomenal baby photographer on the mainland of Vancouver, Canada. I want Amanda, along with her two precious daughters Olivia and Sophia, to ALWAYS remember their FRONTLINE heritage and know that a space is there to be filled by each of them. And my niece Krista Bella, who is the most BRILLIANT artist ever, who uses her gift of generosity to always love everyone.

Their mama Sharon (my Stephen's sister) has paved the way, loving Jesus right on the FRONTLINE of service. Sharon ministers to everyone everywhere she goes!! She also leads worship EVERY SUNDAY with her loving husband Alan on guitar and her precious son Joshua on the piano. FRONTLINE WOMEN RUN GENERATIONALLY!!!!

You, FRONTLINE WARRIOR GIRL, are leading and leaving YOUR LEGACY to those who are with you and behind you. I love how my Sister-heart friend Pastor Pam Hart (Victory Church, Great Falls Montana) always says, "FINISH STRONG."

She is one of the most committed FRONTLINE Women I know who refuses to finish weak... even in her darkest moments, and she's had many. She rises right back up to strength on the FRONTLINE every-single-time.

FINISH STRONG BEAUTIFUL FRONTLINE WOMAN. YOU ARE STRONG, DANGEROUS & INVALUABLE!

I Believe In You Always. I pray now in the name of our Master Jesus Christ that excitement for what's ahead envelops you. I pray happiness overtakes you and your heart of gratitude paves the way to the miraculous.

Big Loves, LaCinda xox

I'm thanking you, God, from a full heart, I'm writing the book on your wonders. I'm whistling, laughing, and jumping for joy; I'm singing your song, High God.

Psalm 9:1 (MSG)

FRONTLINE DISCUSSION

What was the most powerful moment of revelation while spending this time together with FRONTLINE WOMEN?

What area do you feel you've gotten the strongest in?

What can you be grateful for right now, in the hardest circumstance you are facing? On my give-up-day, I realized how being thankful for my nurses, good medical care, my warm housecoat, quarters for the wall phone, good hospital food, and so much more gave me the freedom to be happy, regardless of the hurtful season I was in. What have you not been noticing?

Thinking back, can you see how God's happiness has brought you strength? Can you see the connection to gratitude and happiness?

I want you to experience happiness even in your tough FRONTLINE times, and you CAN with practice. Begin a Gratitude Journal. Be committed to recount your most grateful moment of the day. Do whatever it takes to make gratitude a part of who you are, not something you force yourself to do. (#FRONTLINEGRATITUDE)

FRONTLINE PRAYER

I thank You, God, for Your strength that comes from HAPPINESS and laughter! Help me to be grateful with eyes to see blessings everywhere, regardless of my most difficult circumstances! This FRONTLINE life can be tough but it is also full of so many amazing moments of JOY and blessings.

I pray now for my tribe, my next generation, and I hold... (add names below) up to You, and I'm trusting You to help me influence them, minister to them and lead them to the FRONTLINE!

In Jesus Name, AMEN.

1.

2.

3.

4.

5.

FRONTLINE CONFESSION

I'm NOT a give up woman! I am a FRONTLINE GENERATIONAL INFLUENCER. The evil one may hunt me down but I will NEVER surrender!

I rest under the shadow of my Master Jesus Christ. I see the good all around me and I'm grateful for God's blessings that surround my life.

I LAUGH—A LOT! I see beauty, joy, love and a positive faith-filled voice speaks love through me!

SCRIPTURES TO BUILD YOUR FAITH

Proverbs 17:22; Philemon 1:7

1 Thessalonians 5:13; Galatians 5:22

Nehemiah 8:10; Psalm 40:1-6